T0146910

What Were Men

What Were Men

Joseph Lee

WHAT WERE MEN

Scripture quotations marked NASB are taken from the New American Standard Bible®, Copyright © 1960, 1962, 1963, 1968, 1971, 1972, 1973, 1975, 1977, 1995 by The Lockman Foundation. Used by permission.

iUniverse books may be ordered through booksellers or by contacting:

iUniverse
1663 Liberty Drive
Bloomington, IN 47403
www.iuniverse.com
1-800-Authors (1-800-288-4677)

ISBN: 978-1-5320-2633-1 (sc)
ISBN: 978-1-5320-2634-8 (e)

Library of Congress Control Number: 2017910503

Print information available on the last page.

iUniverse rev. date: 01/30/2018

The best way to succeed is to love what you do.
If you don't try anything new, you'll never succeed.
Decide to live the best, most lovely, adventurous, and romantic life you can.

Contents

Introduction vii

Part 1: The Lovely Life

1 Love For Melanie 3
2 Love For Lala 7
3 Longing in the Spirit 14
4 Melanie—The Goddess of Wisdom 18
5 Temptation from Lala 24

Part 2: The Adventurous Life

6 Lost My Chastity 31
7 Apprentice in Germany 36
8 A Tempestuous Thursday 40
9 Piecework 42

Part 3: The Work Life

10 Homo Sapiens 47
11 A Disgusting Event 52
12 King of the Coal Hewers 57
13 Improving My German 63

Part 4: The Romantic Life

 14 A Beautiful Bride Uses a Sink as a Chamber Pot 67
 15 Korea's First Gold at the Olympics—1972 Munich 72
 16 The Poker Champion Presbyter Baeg 74
 17 Under an Assumed Name 77
 18 Three Encounters with the Angel of Death 80

Part 5: The Tragic Life

 19 The Shock of a Quick Dismissal 93
 20 Misfortune.. 97
 21 A Silly Suicide 99
 22 Why a Private Apartment? 101
 23 Petrified Jung..103

Part 6: The Determined Life

 24 A Third Journey..109
 25 The Genius Melanie in Oxford.................................. 112
 26 Honeymoon Baby.. 117
 27 German Scholarship 119
 28 Das Rigorosum and Back to Korea 124

Introduction

What is your situation now? Life is a once-in-a-lifetime opportunity, and depending on your attitude you can live your opportunity as you wish.

This is the story of a young Korean man who courageously unfolds his will for the future, thinks positively, and practices all things together. More than seven thousand Koreans were guest workers in West Germany from 1964 to 1975. I was one. I went there to work in mines on a three-year contract. I wanted to save money because I wanted to earn a doctorate. After my three-year contract, I took a university language course and worked as a miner for almost another year. It was a very tough year—school during the day and work in the mines at night, but I was very happy. After passing the German exam, I was awarded a degree and was qualified to pursue a doctorate.

I am particularly grateful to all those who settled in Germany and became experts in various fields. They live as well as their counterparts do in other countries, including Korea. I believe that the best thing we can do is live life the best we can and make it worthwhile.

Sociologists study laborers who move to other countries and how they adapt to different societies. Korea and Germany, for instance, are very different cultures, and the lives of Koreans in Germany were tough, but my colleagues and I survived our mining jobs and helped one another. Sociologists concluded that Korean workers in Germany were more diligent and sincere and smarter than workers there from any other country.

The male and female protagonists are sincere figures in a liberal, democratic society. Their lives, worlds, religious views, and philosophies of life are lessons we can all learn and appreciate.

I want to bear witnesses to the will and the ways of Koreans in Korea and abroad who act boldly in spite of difficulties they face.

Thank you, readers.

Part 1

The Lovely Life

Chapter 1

Love For Melanie

Melanie was the Christian name of Young Soon Lee, a descendant of the Lee dynasty in Korea. Her father was the only prince of the twenty-third dynasty; his only child was Melanie. Melanie's father had died at age twenty-seven, so there was no hope for a male successor. Because Melanie's grandfather abused her and her mother, her mother decided to move with Melanie, an infant at the time, to Seoul.

Life was hard for a single mother with no money. She worked in a market with Melanie at her side. Melanie was gentle, obedient, virtuous, kind, and healthy. She helped her mother at the store when she was not in school. She would take care of customers when her mother used the ladies' room. Melanie had the habit of giving customers more than they wanted and charged little, but her mother did not blame her for that; she was only helping others.

Melanie was a genius all the way from grade school to college; she always earned the highest grades. She and I studied at the same state university for teachers; she studied English, and I studied Korean. We met occasionally on campus, but we didn't really know each other that well.

In 1969, Korea was still a poor country. The unemployment rate was over 30 percent, and the per capita income was just $300. In those days, many students had no money for lunch, but Melanie's mother worked hard to make sure Melanie had three meals a day.

Melanie and I wanted to teach, but we knew it would be hard to find jobs in our fields. Despite our difficult circumstances, she got a job teaching English at the Lily Girls High School, in Seoul, and after I served for three years as a lieutenant in the army—that was my compulsory military service—I got a job as a teacher of Korean at the Seoul Hero Boys High School. We did well and were rewarded medals for our work, but even then, we had not properly met.

Once a year, Korean students go on study tours to museums, Buddhist temples, national cemeteries where our historic heroes lie, or simply to the mountains. Melanie and I happened to go at the same time with our students to the Song Nee Mountain and the biggest Buddhist temple in East Asia.

Along with our students, Melanie and I climbed the mountain together; it was our first time in each other's company since our university days. We felt very comfortable together. Our colleagues became jealous when they saw our interest in each other.

But that's when the fight occurred. On the same day, students from the Ac Dong Boys High School in Seoul went to the mountain. That school had many famous sports clubs—judo, tae kwon do, soccer, handball, weight lifting, fencing, and so on. The students there had a reputation for being aggressive.

The Ac Dong students left for the mountain later than did our students, and they met our students as we were descending the mountain. The Ac Dong students were envious of the fact that my Hero students were in the company of the Lily students, and some of the Ac Dong students started fighting with mine. My students fought gallantly, but they were losing ground. Melanie was hugging her girls, who were trembling in fear.

I didn't see any teachers from Ac Dong school, so I tried to stop the fighting by myself, but the Ac Dong boys kept fighting. "Stop!" I yelled at them. But they just rudely taunted me. One student tried to knock me down, and another tried some tae kwon do on me. I am a third degree in judo and a fifth degree in tae kwon do and had been a lieutenant in the special forces paratroopers. I twisted the arm of one of my attackers and forced him to the ground, and I gave another a side kick. Everything happened so fast. My second attacker fell down a slope about ten feet.

The battle was over. I climbed down to the boy and discovered his arm was broken and his face was bloody. An Ac Dong teacher finally arrived, and I explained to him what had happened. Melanie bandaged the boy as best she could with strips from her slip. I found some branches and tied my jacket between them to form a stretcher for the boy; his classmates carried him to the hospital.

After our return, Melanie and I had to write reports for the superintendent. The parents of the wounded boy had lodged a complaint against me and demanded that I be fired. A disciplinary committee was established, and it took three months to reach a verdict. The leader of the Ac Dong high school and I had to resign. Nonetheless, those at the Lily Girls High School were happy that I had been there, and they were happy that Melanie and I had developed a relationship.

That confrontation convinced the city superintendent of educational affairs in Seoul to make sure that students visited the different places at different times; he wanted to avoid such brawls.

I was angry with the educational authority; they refused to realize that students could indeed attack teachers and that the teachers weren't respected by them or their superiors or the legal system. Teachers should not have to suffer that way. All this discouraged me; I lost the courage to teach with love and enthusiasm. But I had found my true love. Melanie and I were together as much as we could be. The feeling I had for her was the same thing I felt when I listen to the "Morning Mood" of Grieg's E-flat major Peer Gynt suite No. 1, Op. 46-I. This musical play is based on Norwegian folk songs. Heinrich Ibsen had asked Grieg to write the score for his story, and the result expresses the beauty and musical history of Norway.

Peer Gynt, the main character, is a ridiculous dreamer, braggart, and adventurer; he is uncontrollably ambitious and roves the world. He has betrayed his lover, Solveig. He sells his soul to the daughter of the devil and goes to Africa to trade slaves. After earning big bucks, he falls in love with the daughter of a chief, but she betrays him. Peer returns home to settle his debt with the devil, and he dies in Solveig's arms.

"I would not want to live like Solveig," Melanie would tell me. "But my darling, our love trip to Song Nee Mountain brought us together. You showed strength and bravery there. I swear eternal love to you. Please kiss and hug me."

"Yes, Melanie," I said, "I also swear eternal love. Let us keep our dream forever."

Because I was shorter than she was, I had to rise up a bit to kiss her gently on her forehead. Her scent was so pleasant, mysterious, and sexy.

The Chinese classical philosopher Mencius (372–289 BC) had a profound influence on Korean culture and tradition, said that humans should be wise(仁 ren), just(義 yi), courteous(禮 li), and intelligent(智 zhi). Melanie was all four.

Chapter 2

Love For Lala

In July 1970, I quit teaching and went to West Germany as a guest worker. My weekends began on Saturday at one o'clock, and that's when I would study German. It seemed that even in summer, the skies were always overcast and the air was foul, which gave me headaches. I was also always worried about my future.

But I persisted; learning requires that. I had been through tough times before, and I wanted to earn a doctorate for my sake and Melanie's sake. I remember sitting in my room staring out into the dismal rain and seeing her beautiful eyes.

Mr. Lee, an assistant interpreter, came into my room. "Mr. Lee, come along quickly," he ordered me militarily.

"Brother Lee, but I'm studying German. Please—"

Koreans call people who are just a little older "brother" or "sister." He laughed. "Come on. We're going to Dusseldorf, to see Brother Park. Come on." I was uneasy. Brother Park's lover lived in Dusseldorf. But I was curious. "Yes, gladly," I said.

He and I took the intercity train to Dusseldorf. No one asked for our tickets. I asked Brother Lee, "Why has no one checked our tickets?"

"Germans are honest people," he said.

"Then why did we buy tickets?"

"Because they are occasionally checked. If you don't have a

ticket, you could be fined twenty times its value. Very few do not buy tickets."

How much faith Germans had in their constitutional state.

We left from Bochum, a small station, passed through Essen and Duisburg, and arrived in Dusseldorf, where the station was full of people. Many of them were Turks, Brother Lee told me.

I saw many Turks with sharp facial features and mustaches. They looked both Western and Asian with their thick, dark eyebrows, long noses, thick lips, and curly hair and beards. Many had strong physiques. They would gather at the train station. Korea and Turkey are brothers. Turkey sent troops to fight the Communists during the Korean War, and they lost many soldiers there.

Brother Lee ran to a pay phone. "Hello! Is Brother Park there? … Yes, yes. We're at the station," he said to someone.

We sat on a bench and waited for about an hour. Brother Lee and I discussed many things. All Korean students read *The Fall of the Third State* and *The Miracle on the Rhine*. Dusseldorf, he said, was the capital city of Nordrheine-Westphalia. I said that Karl Marx must have worked there, but he did not respond. Karl Marx, a Communist, was a taboo topic in South Korea, but in Germany, his books were widely available.

Brother Park and a wonderful Korean woman came into the hall. Brother Lee and I stood open-mouthed.

"This is Mr. Lee. The other you already know," Park said to his lover.

"I'm pleased to meet you. I'm Giesela. How are you, Mr. Lee?"

Giesela was about six feet tall. Her face was narrow and elongated, and her nose was high, nicely flat and round as is usual with Korean women. Her teeth were very white, and her lips were painted only subtly. In recent decades, Korean women have grown taller than Korean men; people say that is because their mothers fed them more, but Korean mothers favor their sons. She had long, gleaming black hair and was wearing a snug-fitting silver blouse and violet skirt that reached to the floor but followed the shape of her legs. She reminded me a little of Queen Beatrix. I had never seen such a beautiful woman. *My Melanie should also wear such beautiful clothes,* I thought. *She would look beautiful as well. But for that, I will need a lot of money.*

We went to the parking garage; she went in alone. Approximately five minutes later, she drove up in a white Mercedes-Benz and opened the door.

"Gentlemen, please get in," she said.

"Come along," said Brother Park.

We drove off and crossed the Rhine; we headed west. She stopped beside a small but pretty five-floor place called Hotels am Rhein. At the entrance, they chatted briefly with another woman who introduced herself as Lala Steinberg. She was also Korean and owned the hotel. I compared the two women secretly while we greeted each other.

Park and Lee gave their names, but I only bowed. Lala looked like Giesela's twin. She looked at me with a strange look, but when I looked at her right, she smiled.

They told us they were old friends and had had another friend, Yoyo Huh, since primary school. They had attended school together through university. Because their parents were all neighbors, they were like sisters, and they called each other sisters.

"Please come in. We'll eat and drink and have a party."

"Mr. Lee has come to Germany just a week ago, but his German is quite good. He taught in a high school. Let's call the old Lee number one, and the new Lee number two, okay? Okay."

Everyone laughed.

"Good evening Lee One and Two."

"Welcome, Mr. Lee Two."

Lala lived in a small house behind the hotel. The house had been built with beams and plaster in between and looked old, but the inside was very modern. The living room contained an expensive Arabic rug, golden lamps, and a silver chandelier. Many decorative plates and silver glasses were in a glass cabinet.

Lala had been married to a man named Ulrich Steinberg. He had been a patient in the university clinic where Lala worked as a nurse. Ulrich fell in love at first sight with her and proposed to her. Of course she had refused; it was unthinkable for a virgin to marry a divorced or widowed man, and Ulrich had two sons and a daughter from a previous marriage. Stepchildren scared Koreans; the culture offers many cautionary tales about such situations.

But Ulrich, the owner of the hotel, pushed her to marry him. A Korean proverb says that little strokes fell great oaks. Though her parents had many objections to her marrying a foreigner, Lala trusted in Ulrich's love and finally said yes.

She thought she would win the love of her stepchildren, but the day after their honeymoon, the problems began. The older son and daughter tried to run away, and the younger son refused to talk to her or eat the meals she prepared. All of them refused to go to school. Their marriage was soon unhappy.

For a Korean female, virginity is almost as important as life itself. At that time, it meant social death for a woman to lose her virginity outside marriage. Lala had yet to register as married with the Korean Registry Office, and there was also no family book issued. Under this situation, she was not entitled to compensation under Korean law. Ulrich would not hear of divorce for a while, but he ultimately gave in to her request to divorce.

Lala moved back into the nurses' hospice and worked there, sad but composed. Three months after the divorce, she received a letter telling her that Ulrich had given her the hotel.

Lala broke into tears as she told this story, and Giesela consoled her. When you're young, love is enchanting.

As the evening continued, as the wine was consumed, my longing for my beloved Melanie grew though she was far away. But I looked at Lala, and she smiled at me. She looked even more beautiful than when I had first seen her. She looked seductive, and her eyes were talking love to me. The wine had brought out my animal instinct and inflamed my passion.

But Brother Park put out the fire with the words, "So now we go to bed. The party is over, ladies and gentlemen."

"Thank you, Mrs. Steinberg, for inviting me to this wonderful party," I said. "And I also thank you, Ms. Oh, and you, Brother Park and Brother Lee. Thank you very much, and good night."

They looked at me with open mouths; they had not expected my German to be so good.

Lala gave Giesela and Brother Park one room, and Lee and me One. And Lala said. "I have to give a separate room to the two of You. It is a weekend, so there are not many rooms left. Is it okay, though?" "No problems." We said. We climbed up to the third floor. The room was clean, and we were happy. I took a bath after he did. At midnight, the phone rang. Brother Lee answered and talked for a while. "Wait! I'll be right there," he said. He told me, "Brother Lee, I'll be back tomorrow. Adios, amigo," and he left.

I could not sleep; I thought about my beautiful Melanie, who had said she would love me forever. But there I was in Germany and she was in Korea, and we did not have a firm commitment to each other. I looked out the window at the Rhine River. I tried to pull myself together. My love for Melanie flowed down the Rhine to the North Sea, the Atlantic, the Mediterranean, through the Suez Canal, and into the Indian Ocean. From there, it went into the Pacific Ocean, the China Sea, and finally up the Han River, which flows through Seoul, where my beloved Melanie lived. I dreamed of how our love would flourish when we were back together.

My happy thoughts were interrupted by the phone. "Hello. This is Lee Two."

"This is not Mrs. Steinberg but Lala. Is Mr. Lee One there?"

"No, he has gone out. I do not know where."

"All the better. Do you want a glass of wine with me, Mr. Lee Two?"

I hesitated, but the thought of her sweet face and beautiful figure won me over.

"Please come, Mr. Lee Two. I'd like to talk with you."

"Well, good. Yes, Where shall I come, my dear?"

I felt a cold sweat. *Is my love for Melanie noble and true?* I was in trouble, but I rationalized my way out of it. I wanted to enjoy the moment. To be a hero, of course, you need to know how to enjoy your time with beautiful women. My libido soared.

When I got to her room, I had forgotten all about Melanie and Korea. She was waiting at the door and took my hand. In the kitchen was a bottle of wine with a French label. She sat very close to me and took me in her arms. She was bigger than me and three years older. She kissed me.

"Lala, I would like some of your wine."

"Yeah, me too," she said and let me go. "It's a Bordeaux that cost eight hundred francs."

"How much is that in marks?" I asked.

"About two hundred."

"Expensive!"

"Yes, of course, but it's my favorite. I have saved it for a very special guest. I will trust you tonight with my body, soul, and spirit. To our health and our love."

We finished three bottles of that wine. Lala stood and undressed. Her body was simply magnificent. I could barely breathe. I let her do what she wanted with me, and my instincts took over. She moaned while we made passionate love.

God created human beings in his own image, male and female. My masculinity connected with Lala's femininity, but it was uncomfortable doing so on a chair.

"Let's go to bed, my dear," I said softly.

In her room, we would sip wine and let it flow into each other's mouths. My instincts had not been satisfied, so she found a new way to satisfy them. She knew more than I did about making love; she was an erotic woman.

"You'll find out what it's like to be with a real woman," she told me.

"Mr. Lee Two, wake up," she said the next morning at ten thirty. "The others are waiting for you for breakfast."

When I went downstairs, Park, Lee, and their respective partners were at the table. I was confused because of the events of the previous night, but Lala was composed. The others stared at me with strange eyes. I was ashamed because I had had sex with her, but I didn't mention that. Lala looked at me lovingly.

After breakfast, Brother Lee and I returned to Bochum. Lala had told me that she wanted to visit me the next weekend.

On the train, I pondered my situation wth Lala. I didn't know if I loved her, while I knew I loved Melanie. But my intimate encounter with Lala was unique as well as unexpected. On the other hand, I had committed a big sin against Melanie, God, and my parents, and I felt guilty. I vowed to be loyal to Melanie forever after.

My passionate time with Lala had drained me physically and mentally. I had gladly experienced it, but my superego told me not to be so weak willed. Before going to sleep, I said softly but firmly, "Melanie, I swear I will behave." But in my sleep, a voice said, "You liar! You have become dirty. You have lost your beloved Melanie. She does not want to see you, you Korean Don Juan!" In my dream, I couldn't breathe. I was in a grave. I cried. Melanie had gone off with another man. I screamed, but no one heard me.

I woke up and remembered Psalm 51. Guilt tightened my chest. I did not want to imitate David. I cried at the thought. I wanted to confess my sin as in Psalm 51: "Have mercy on me, God, in your goodness and abundant compassion blot out my offense."

Chapter 3

Longing in the Spirit

During my stay in Germany, I always imagined Melanie listening to Grieg's "Morning Mood." I was full of hope and confidence; I wanted to attend university in Germany.

Melanie had sent me a letter and was waiting for my reply. I read it many times because it made me so happy and full of hope, and it made me forget my weakness.

To my sweetheart Joseph,

In August, everyone here in Seoul is tired because of the heat. Even at night, the temperature never drops below 90 degrees Fahrenheit, and it feels like the tropics. I'm taking a training course, a total of 40 days and 240 hours to qualify for a higher position and salary.

How are you, my love?

I have often thought about our future that you have identified with your last letter for me lately. After careful consideration, I have to decide now. I love you so much; I want to marry you before I go to England to take my doctorate. I have also thought to work in Germany as a nurse, but then I would have to learn a new profession and would lose more time.

I think you will like this suggestion: We can initially simply get the papers we need from the registry office and register legally as husband and wife. Then I'll get busy and apply for state scholarships to study abroad. The testing takes place in November. I must take the TOEFL, the Test of English as a Foreign Language, and score at least six hundred out of nine hundred points. I would like to study at Oxford.

This is my suggestion for our future—you and I will be university professors. I will study English didactics; what will you study? How about biology, physics, or communications technology? You could get a doctorate in any of those fields.

Mother wants to know how things are for you in Germany and when you will come to Korea so we can marry. She said, "Although there are many morals to married life, one important one is to not give advice unless it is requested." So you decide, and I will respond if you ask me.

She knows we love each other. She is sad; my father's death, though it was twenty-seven years ago, is still a big loss for her. Mother asked me if we had agreed to marry, and though I did not yet have your answer, I said yes.

My dearest, be careful. A woman I know has two children; her husband died in an industrial accident in Saudi Arabia. I beg you to always think of me and our mother, who is counting on us. I send you all my love and wait longingly for your answer.
Your Melanie.

So Melanie wanted to be my wife; she had never said that before. Her letter showed me her gentle heart. I discovered new sides of her, and I felt such deep love for her. In Korea, women never proposed to men, but Melanie had proposed to me.

I wrote back to her full of joy and hope.

August 19, 1970
To my dearest Melanie

Today is Saturday. On Saturday and Sunday, we do not work in Germany. Actually, I need not get up early, but I woke up out of habit as early as five o'clock.

I drink coffee and write this letter to you in this quiet "Morning Mood." When I read your letter, my body, spirit, and soul became clear. When I think of you, my heart overflows with joy and hope. I sing a song about our love, a children's song in Germany.

> Gold and silver, precious stones
> Most beautiful secret places
> You are mine, I am yours
> You are mine Oh! What could be nicer?

Soon, my older brother will visit you to greet you and your mother. Please give him your birth certificate and family certificate confirmed by the registry office. This must accompany our application for marriage.

We can get married in England or Germany. I want to get married in a cathedral because you're Catholic.

In Korea, I would like to eventually build a two-story house with a lawn and trees. We will have a big dog, a cat, some chickens, and a horse for our children to play with. We will have a garden with flowers and vegetables and every kind of fruit tree.

How many children we will have will depend on you. I gladly would have at least three: two sons and a daughter, or maybe two daughters and a son. You are clever, and you are a genius, so our children will be awesome. I'm so happy that you want to my wife. I promise to always be good to you.

I imagine the sun on your face in the morning. Oh, my sweetheart Melanie, you are my protection, my hope, and the light of my eyes. You govern my sanity, and you teach me love. You're my Alpha and Omega, my whole life.

On Saturday, I mailed the letter and diligently studied German; only if I learned German could I realize my dream with Melanie.

In one dream, I met Melanie.

"Oh my love! How are you?"

"Thank you. I'm fine."

"Yesterday, I did some piecework; that means I was rewarded for my performance only. I have done hard things before such as learning judo and tae kwon do and how to parachute out of a plane. I have learned to endure. Yesterday, I earned forty marks for mining ten tons of coal."

"Forty marks? How much is that in Korean money?"

"Um, eighteen hundred won, I think, my love. But it is not enough."

"Do you love me, my love?"

"Yes, so much!"

"Then do not worry. You're mine now, and my mother, your mother-in-law, prays in church for you every day."

"Yes, I always think of you and your mother. Not your mother, but our mother. But where are you? I cannot you see."

"Here I am, my darling."

"Where? Ah, there you are. Give me your hands."

Ring! Just as I was about to hold Melanie, my alarm woke me.

Chapter 4

Melanie—The Goddess of Wisdom

I received a nice letter from Melanie with the return address, "From Your Wife Young Soon Lee." Her handwriting was neat, tidy, and clean, just as her spirit was.

To my dear husband,

I am a little ashamed because I have already called you my husband. This is my fourth attempt to write to you because it is still so unfamiliar and unnatural for me to address you as my man.

Yesterday afternoon, we visited Older Brother, Father-in-Law Lord, who gave us many pounds of rice, beans, sesame seeds, sesame oil, and beef. My mom and I were receiving gifts for the first time. And Mom rejoices at a gift sent from the house of the in-laws. And Older Brother said that Father-in-Law will send us thirty pounds of rice a month.

Your name and mine are in the family books together, which makes me feel close to you. I slept with the book in my arms, but I could not sleep because of my throbbing mind. Every woman would like to get married and have a family. My heart feels empty because you're not with me.

In the coming semester, I will take the TOEFL exam. I need your support, love, and prayers. I will survive; don't worry.

Darling, you're my man. Though we haven't married yet, we're already a couple. I call myself your parents' daughter-in-law, and I want to get to know them. At the Autumn Festival, I'll visit them.

Last night, my mother had declared our marriage and showed me the family book. She said, "You'll leave me. This is the fate of all women. My sweetheart, I want you to be eternally happy with your husband. Oh my darling, hug me!"

We cried. In order to console her, I told her, "Mama, when I study in England, you shall come to look after our baby. Mom, believe me, he really does consider you his mom."

My beloved! I want to see you. How far are you from. How far away you are! I, your wife, long for you so much.

The weather in Korea this fall is getting cooler. If the harvest is good, many farmers' daughters will get married. In Korean, there is no word for "marry." When women get married, they go to their husbands' homes; when men get married, they bring their wives home. Regardless, I still consider myself married.

It's all like a dream. It is the happiness of every woman to marry a loved one. It's already one in the morning. I'll go to sleep. Come to me when I go to sleep because you're my man. See you soon.

—Your loving wife, Melanie, writes to you on August 28, 1970, from Seoul, Korea.

Yes! We had become one as God had promised. "It is not good that the man should be alone, so I will give him a companion suitable for him." God created a suitable companion for me; Melanie came into this world only for me. Her love is the sum of agape and philia love. How I love her. "That is why a man leaves his father and mother and clings to his wife, and the two of them become one body." This rule is the basis of all family systems; in this way, couples obey God's will.

I want to live with my wife, Melanie, who freely decided to marry me. I sent her two thousand marks in gratitude; it was all I had saved.

On Monday afternoon, I bought food for a whole week—eight pork knuckles, two pounds of beef, bread, cold cuts, and all the ingredients for Korean *kimchee*—cabbage, cucumber, carrots, onions, garlic, and peppers.

In the market, I chatted in my mind with Melanie. She advised me about what to buy. Up to that time, I'd grab whatever I first saw and end up with sour milk, moldy cheese, rotten eggs, rotten fruit, and so on. But in my mind, she taught me to be more careful. In my mind, she spoke to me.

"Darling, are you on a streetcar? We don't have those any longer in Korea."

"Yes, darling, I'm on a streetcar."

"What's over there behind the hill? That high tower? And there's another!"

"Those are where the coal pits are, and they are very deep."

I was carrying four heavy bags of groceries that were hurting my hands and wrists and turning them blue. I had to soak them in warm water and massage them for an hour at home.

When I unpacked my winter clothes from my suitcase, I found an envelope with Melanie's handwriting on it. Inside was a photo of her smiling and leaning against a tree, and a poem.

Before leaving my husband
The man of whom
I have dreamed since childhood

My beloved, my husband wants
tomorrow to travel to a far country
Melanie loves him sincerely
He has come but does not kiss me
but charmed me he wants to separate
from me without us today
our lives have promised
—07/07/1970 written by your wife Melanie

PS: Ruth said, Do not ask me to abandon or forsake you, for wherever you go, I will go. Wherever you lodge, I will lodge. Your people shall be my people, and your God my God. Ruth 1:16–17.

I heard "Morning Mood" as I read her poem. I was motionless. What could I say? When I was leaving for Germany, she didn't come to the airport to say goodbye; she said she had to study for an exam. I thought our love would pass. I had doubted her love, but she had not. She had wanted to be my wife from the outset. She trusted me and put all her hopes in me. She had quoted Ruth, and she loved and lived as Ruth had. I kissed her photo. I planned to buy a photo frame the next day.

I made dinner and tried to learn German by watching the TV my landlord had given me. The picture was bad, but the sound was good. At ten, I went to bed and dreamed of Melanie.

"You, my beloved! Have you really been waiting for me since your childhood?" My face flushed. She did not answer.

"Don't be shy! You are my everything. Are you sorry that we did not have a proper wedding ceremony with a white veil?" I asked.

"No. I do not need a white veil. But I would like to be married in a Catholic church. What do you think?"

"That's proper. Just as you want, it will happen."

"Thank you, my favorite. If I may ask, what denomination do your parents belong to?"

"They have become evangelical recently; before that, they were Buddhist. They're just honest, poor, and pious people. My mother and father know you as a gift from God because you are beautiful, smart, and noble. Visit them soon."

"Yes, I will. They will have grandchildren."

"Thank you, my love. But what I can show your mother, our mother? I have nothing."

"Don't worry. You will get a PhD in Germany, and I will get one in England. That will be a great gift to Mother."

"Melanie, my love, where are you? I cannot see you."

"Here—I'm with you!"

That of course was when my alarm rang. In the afternoon, I wrote my wife a letter.

To my dear wife Melanie

You and I, a couple: I am in a solemn mood; I have no words to tell you how much. September began with rain, and so far, this has not changed. The people here have been around for twelve days with no sun, only clouds. Everything is gray.

Normally, the house is heated only when the temperature is below fifty degrees Fahrenheit, but it is fifty degrees. We Koreans are very cold, and some of us are sick, but the doctor is reluctant to issue sick certificates to us, so we have to work.

So far, I have stayed healthy, and I have worked diligently. Today, I earned eighty marks. I do not write this to brag. I will only say that I have been working very hard despite all the difficulties. I have been creative, and I have solved many problems at work. I've been praised by the company's district overseer, and I am earning a lot of money.

Some Koreans do not like me; I think they are jealous of how much I am earning. There are rumors that I have given money or gifts to especially friendly Germans. Their crooked thoughts are not worth getting nervous about. You know the Korean proverb: when my nephew buys land, I get stomach pains. Or another saying: I hate those who do not give me anything even though I have given them nothing. But I do not hate anyone, and I am not unkind to anyone. I love people.

The window in my room faces west, which is not good for a Korean. I will sweat in summer and freeze in winter. I'll probably not see the sun ever in winter.

Our future house should face south. I want a thoroughbred Korean shepherd, a cat that will hide in the fields, and hens and chicks. Our children should grow up surrounded by nature. They will grow up knowing why it rains and snows, and that there are people of different colors in the world, which is God's unique creation that he protects.

My love! Yesterday afternoon, I found your picture and your poem in that suitcase. It was a big surprise I had not expected.

Thank you so much for your poem; it gives me strength and confidence. Your smile makes me happy. I promise to never forget it.

> My dearest
> Someday, you will blossom like a lotus flower
> We have prophesied that you'll be my wife
> We really are a lovely couple
> As we predicted, our marriage will last for eternity
> Love and trust watches over us
> Love blooms for lovers who reaping the fruits of love
> I write this letter to you on September 10, 1970.

Chapter 5

Temptation from Lala

I had become accustomed to my work as a miner, and I felt at home in Germany. But when I had to work a different shift, I found it hard to sleep during the day. And I changed shifts every week.

The head of the training department, the company's chief production officer, praised me many times and suggested I work in his group after my training. And so I learned the company handbook by heart.

I wanted to learn more German, so I asked someone for a newspaper one time, and he gave me a tabloid. On the front page was a picture of a naked woman with big breasts, something I had never seen in Korea. I read the story and discovered the woman was an Italian stripper who was running for parliament. I couldn't believe it. I knew that German was difficult to learn, but the German in newspapers was very confusing in that it didn't adhere to the grammar rules I was learning. It took me most of the morning to read four pages of that tabloid. The person who gave me the paper tried to help me read and pronounce German, which I found very difficult because of the umlauts and other marks that affected pronunciation.

"Practice makes champions, Mr. Lee," he told me. And so I did practice. He was a good teacher. He and I would get off work at 1:00, and he would teach me until 1:40. "Thank you, Mr. Master," I told him repeatedly.

I memorized many vocabulary words on my own, and I studied the rules of grammar. I would walk outside to keep from falling asleep as I studied German. Once when I was doing that, I didn't notice that it had started to rain until my textbook got all wet.

Back in my room, I was making tea when I heard a knock on my door.

"Mr. Lee, two ladies wish to visit you," the housemaster said.

Two women? Who could that be? But when I smelled a familiar perfume even through the door, I knew it was Lala, but I didn't know who was with her. I put my photo of Melanie on the table as a sign that I already had a beautiful lover.

I opened the door. Two women stood in the hallway.

"Mr. Lee. This home does not allow women," the housemaster said. "Your guests have to leave in thirty minutes."

I didn't know what to do.

"Mr. Lee, do you want us to just stand here?"

"You can come in, please." I felt embarrassed.

Lala said, "This is Yoyo. Yoyo, this is Mr. Lee, my friend."

"Hi, Mr. Lee," Yoyo said. "I'm glad to meet you."

Yoyo was as beautiful as Lala. They entered the room and saw that my roommate Siegfried's bed was not made.

"Please sit," I said.

"You're learning German, Mr. Lee?" asked Lala after seeing my book. She looked closely at Melanie's picture, and she stiffened. My heart was beating. I had promised myself not to see Lala again for Melanie's sake.

"Have you eaten?" Lala asked.

"No," I replied.

"Then let's go to Dusseldorf perhaps with a friend of yours for Yoyo."

I have to find a friend for Yoyo? Yes, of course I had some friends, but which one would I introduce to Yoyo? Lala was still peering darkly at Melanie's photo.

"Okay," Lala said. "Let's go, Yoyo. Mr. Lee, please?"

I could not decide. I had not yet learned all the vocabulary, so I could not go with her to Dusseldorf. I remembered our passion the last time, but my superego slowed me down. I didn't know what to do.

But Lala showed me what she wanted. She took my hands and dragged me out of my room. She was driving a '65 Mercedes-Benz. I looked out the window with great anxiety as we drove at 130 kilometers per hour.

"The speed on the highway in Germany is unlimited, Mr. Lee," Lala said.

We got to the hotel in an hour. It was only my second visit, but the living room was as inviting as I remembered it. I sat on the sofa, and in came Brother Park and Giesela from the dining room. I was shocked.

"Why did you come so late? It's seven o'clock," said Brother Park as he smiled at Giesela.

The women began to drink, and they must have been very thirsty. They drank like horses after a race—four glasses within half an hour. I drank only two glasses, while Brother Park had three. We ate some hard rolls and cheese with the wine.

I felt very uncomfortable while the others seemed to have a good time. Lala and I exchanged glances, and I had to fight myself. I felt guilty. *How can I escape?* I had left my jacket in my room, so I had no money to get back by myself to Bochum. I sat in the corner of the room and would have stayed there all night if I hadn't needed to use the toilet. I gathered my courage and told myself, *Just stand up and go!*

"You want to stay here with Lala, is that it?"

Do I want to sleep with her? My superego and id were fighting between escaping and loving. I knew how great Lala was in bed. My desires battled my conscience. I wanted to stay even if it meant I would fry in hell. I had lost track of how much I had drunk. My mind seemed to work, but my body obeyed me only reluctantly.

"Mr. Lee, sleep well. We'll see you at breakfast tomorrow," said Brother Park.

I heard his words with only half an ear; my thoughts were clouded. I ran after him and stopped him in the garden. "Brother Park, I need your help—a hundred marks to get back to Bochum."

He looked at Giesela, who was staring at me in horror. "Mr. Lee, I have no money with me. Giesela has some money, I think. But you'd better tonight sleep here and go home tomorrow."

Lala came out of the house and approached us with a worried look on her face. She called on Brother Park and Giesela to convince me to stay the night.

"Mr. Lee," Brother Park said, "please go back to the house. I'll see you tomorrow morning. Adieu!" He went to his car as Lala pulled me back into the house. Yoyo was not there. Lala was lost in thought. *The wife of this man is clearly in Korea. But I want to have a baby with this man. In Germany now, there are many babies without dads.*

I could no longer control myself. My instincts took over. We had wild sex that night. We made love all night long. We fell asleep when the birds started singing.

I had sinned against my wife for the second time. I really did not know how to free myself from my passion.

Part 2

The Adventurous Life

Chapter 6

Lost My Chastity

March 1, 1970, was a Korean national holiday that celebrated the country's independence from Japan in 1919.

On that day, three hundred of us took a train from Seoul to a dreary, dismal coal-mining region in Korea's Kangwon Province for training. We were going to Germany to work as apprentices in the coal mines. On the train, we played cards, drank, and sang all night.

We three hundred formed up at the training center, the Korean Development Center for the Overseas Service (KDCOS). Because of the dense fog, the mood was murky. Our hair was damp with the mist, and some faces were blue with cold; not all had brought warm clothes. A forty-year-old man addressed us informally.

"Dear friends, welcome. My name is Gong, and I'm directing the center. We will train you to become miners. To make money and live a better life, you will have to work hard. Always follow what your boss says during training. And pay particular attention to the rain in the pit. Um … er …"

"Ha, ha, ha! What are you saying? Rain in the pit? Are you crazy?" those who heard him yelled.

"Ha, ha, yes. That sounds ridiculous. But it really does rain there. If you see rain, run. Otherwise, you'll die, and your girlfriends will marry your best friends. The rain I'm talking about is carbon. Coal dust. It will fall very gently at first, but then it will pour and kill you if you do not pay attention to it. No more Germany! Do not laugh! Do not think! Just learn how to mine well, you moles!"

The director returned to his office without saying goodbye.

A short, fat man with a white helmet yelled, "Dear friends! I am an instructor here. We will divide you into ten groups so we can assign you your equipment and a place to sleep."

We were very uneasy. By their speech, we could tell they were apathetic and bored. Nevertheless, he continued, "Uh … ladies and gentlemen—"

We whistled and howled. "Ridiculous guy! Ladies and gentlemen? How silly! Don't make us laugh! Away with you, you pig." People were right; there were no women around. Some people in the front line heckled the man, who could not make himself heard. He fell silent and looked away from us. He bit his lower lip. He waited for silence, and he had to wait several minutes.

"As our captain said, you are moles. I call you something worse than that—mole dung. You'll dig or die. Attention! Form up in ten lines. When I say, 'Front row, sit!' the front row will sit. Got that, you moles? Then I'll say, 'Second row, sit!' and the second row better sit."

We tried to get in lines as he yelled at us. "The devil take you all, you wretches! Third row, sit! Fourth row, sit! You moles are nothing but rat shit. Lassa!"

He became so angry that he threw his helmet. It hit someone, a big man, in the last row and broke his nose. They took him to the doctor.

An hour later, he came back with a thick white mask; he looked like Zorro. The head trainer gave him a sideways glance; eyes bored into each other. Both were furious.

"Have you nothing to tell me?" asked the man with the broken nose.

"What can I tell you? Shit!"

People were curious to see how the situation would evolve. It evolved quickly. The injured man grabbed the trainer, lifted him over his head, and threw him into the river at the edge of the courtyard. The man swam back.

The event gathered police, fire officials, and executives, who were furious. All of us had to kneel in the yard without lunch. We stayed there until five o'clock that afternoon. The police captain supervised the distribution of our equipment and assigned us to living quarters.

After dinner, the police deprived us of sleep and hit us with truncheons until well into the night. The apprentices were beaten into docile submission. The next morning, we apprentices were half-dead. But not me.

I was only an apprentice, but the KDCOS appointed me treasurer of the apprentices. As such, I had to collect a total of nine million won—three hundred times thirty thousand won, the total cost of our training. Why they chose me I didn't know.

I myself had been treated well since I had arrived there, and I later spoke with the director of the training center, the directors of the mine, the police captain, and several other dignitaries of the village. I had lunches and dinners with them.

On the second day, I visited the mines we would be working in with the chief of the training center and with the head trainer. I saw my first coal pit though I was familiar with anthracite, which we used for cooking in Korea. Up until then, I had no idea where it had come from.

During the tour, I asked to enter the great pit, which was called Hex, so I could see how the apprentices were doing there. What I discovered was that they worked in miserable conditions.

On the evening of the third day, I demanded a joint meeting with the director, the directors of all the mines, and others to demand an improvement in the way the apprentices were treated. The director of the center opened the meeting in an uncertain voice. "I welcome you all warmly to this meeting tonight, which was not convened because of me but because of the special demand of the apprentices. Please Mr. Lee, what is it?"

"Thank you very much, Mr. Director. My dear sir, what I want to tell you is very important to the apprentices. We want the following demands fulfilled immediately without exception. First, the motels in which we are staying. We want warm water for showers. Next, we need more-nutritious food to be able to endure the heavy work. We need warm blankets. I gave enough money to each motel for this.

"Second, the masters of all mines should have college degrees. Third, the mines should train the apprentices, not simply expect them to work as if they were in a normal mine. We are beginners. Please teach us basic safety rules and the basic skills we need for mining. Each mine has been paid for this as required.

"Fourth, the course for teaching German should start immediately. We will have another meeting in a week about these matters. Thank you for your attention."

The ten group spokesmen clapped and cheered, but management was speechless and shocked that I had come forth with such demands! But in the end, they decided to meet our demands, and we celebrated with women and liquor.

The apprentices who had come to Germany were from different social classes but were educated. Of the 300, 184 had bachelor's degrees, and twenty-three had master's degrees. All the others had at least graduated from high school. I knew this because as their secretary, I had all that information.

In 1970, Korea was progressing economically, but the differences between the rich and the poor were great. In those days, if you wanted a good life, you had to already have wealth or at least influential family members in the political or business worlds. You needed connections to get jobs, secure permits, and so on.

By the third week of training, seventy apprentices had left; the work was hard. At the beginning of the fourth week, 110 apprentices were gone, and at the end of the fourth week, there were only ninety apprentices there; we were all apprentices who had not come with special, influential pressure. Three of my good friends with whom I had gone to university were among us.

Since it didn't make sense to keep up the entire training operations for the ninety apprentices, the rest of the training was canceled. We left with what we had learned. I returned to Seoul.

I cannot remember my training very well. During that time, almost every evening, I was invited by the director or the chief of police or inspectors from Seoul to visit the Rose, a place where we could buy rice wine and beautiful women. I fell asleep each time with the landlady, a twenty-eight-year-old unmarried woman, but I didn't have to pay. That was the first time I slept with a woman. Until then, I had never even hugged a woman or held a woman's hand.

On the first night there, I was so drunk that I didn't realize what she was having me do until it was much too late, but it taught me what sleeping with a woman was all about. During those four weeks, I swam in alcohol when I wasn't swimming in her femininity. I ended up losing four weeks as well as my virginity.

Chapter 7

Apprentice in Germany

One Sunday afternoon, forty-eight apprentices and I rode a bus from the airport in Dusseldorf to Bochum-Gerthe, which belonged to the Eschweiler Mine Company. On the grounds were six barracks side by side separated by a grassy field populated by blackbirds. It was a hot, cloudless, and calm day. Before us stood a large, fat man, and next to him, a Korean with a peaceful face.

"Hi, Gluck auf, Kumpel, welcome to our home. My name is Wolfgang Esser. Mr. Kim will translate what I say into Korean. I'm the warden. I think you are all hungry. We have for you ready German food—sausage and cabbage to fill your stomachs. We will explain the house rules and show you to your rooms. Mr. Kim, please translate."

"Here, we always say 'Gluck auf' to each other. It is the way we greet colleagues. Gluck means luck, and auf means from above."

The man looked satisfied, and I could understand his German, but the interpretation was bad. We then learned the house rules. At the same time, two women came with a large vessel of food that smelled appetizing. Mr. Kim, however, paid no attention; he went on talking almost an hour. Kim emphasized that it was an absolute must to obey the commands of our superiors. He explained that the master had worked for three years, but his yellow helmet was the same as ours; he was like a master sergeant in the military. The overseer, who wore a white helmet, was like a second lieutenant. The overseer was like a major, and the chief overseer was like a colonel.

As he was talking, the women said, "The food is getting cold!"

Kim looked at the women and acted shocked. "When did you come?"

"You haven't seen us?" they asked.

"No, I haven't."

"Okay. Can we serve the food?"

"Yes, do that."

The apprentices lined up, and the women gave each a sausage and sauerkraut on a paper plate. The Koreans sat in groups of two or three on the lawn and tried to eat the unfamiliar food because they were hungry, but not everyone could finish their meals. Even on the Air France flight to Germany, they couldn't stomach the greasy, oily European food and longed for sharp, fiery, Korean food. Most of them ate the sausage but not all their sauerkraut; however, my friends and I enjoyed it; we had no problem with German food.

"This tastes good. May I have more, my dear lady?" I asked.

"Wonderful! You speak good German. Very good. Eat as much as you want," said the woman as she gave me two more sausages and more sauerkraut, and I ate it all.

After lunch, we were assigned to our barracks. My roommate was Siegfried, who was thirty-one and married to a nurse. Our room had just one window, and the view was very bleak—I could see only a tree-covered hill behind piles of gravel. The clouds, however, were very beautiful. I saw Melanie's face in them, very clean and attractive. I tried to hug her, but she vanished. That night, I talked to her in a dream.

"Hello my dear Melanie, I'm back."

"How can you so quickly again be there?"

"Do you love me, Melanie?"

"Yes! You are my love, my life. You are my everything. I come every night to you in my dreams because we love each other so.

We need every night together. Come to me and talk to me, I hear everything you say. Oh! I love you so much."

"I am in your eyes, and you are in my eyes. My lips are forever yours. My heart beats just for you. My soul needs you, and my body governs your mind. I cannot live without you. I love you. Kiss me."

"Yes, darling, I kiss you and hug you. I also cannot live without you. I want to forever with you. I love you so much. Thank you. Because your heart beats strong, I can sleep. Thanks for your broad chest, which I can throw my whole self on. I love you forever."

"Dear, but where are you? I cannot see you."

Ring. Again, the alarm clock stopped me from embracing her. I got up and went to the washroom. My second day in Germany was starting.

We waited for the buses to take us to work. The bus arrived on time, but some of the apprentices were late. The bus driver waited patiently for a few minutes, but then, he started the bus and drove slowly with the door open. He stopped about twenty yards away for the apprentices who came running. He didn't wait for all the apprentices; he drove off, and in about ten minutes, we reached the place where we would train.

A German master started teaching us the fundamentals—we practiced cutting tree trunks, which was not easy to do; it required strength and concentration. We had to learn how to do it if we wanted to earn money. "Learning how to cut wood is necessary if you want to construct a safe mine," the master told us.

I practiced diligently, and I was praised for cutting boards accurately by the masters; others were not that successful—their boards were quite crooked.

At noon, we stopped work for ninety minutes of German lessons that we were told would last for only eight weeks.

On the way back, everyone in the bus fell asleep except me; I studied German intently; I had to improve my skills in the language if I wanted to study in that country. I wanted to be perfect. I focused on learning new words every day.

After dinner, I wrote letters to my parents and to my love. That was how my second day in Germany ended.

We continued learning how to cut the wood we needed to brace the roofs of the mines we would work in, and we had to do that very accurately to avoid a coalface from collapsing on us.

During the fourth week, we went underground with Mr. Park, a Korean who was thirty-four and had come to Germany in 1964 to train as an engineer. He was a well-bred man and an academic, and he spoke good English. He was a very good leader. He told us about coal in Germany; the country had more than twenty-four billion tons of it, and that would last more than a hundred years. Coal was used there mainly to generate electricity in power plant. Pollution caused by coal burning was precisely and strictly limited by law.

I believed that practice makes perfect. I wanted a good life with Melanie, and that meant I had to work hard and learn as much as I could in the mines as a guest worker.

At that time in West Germany, about twenty thousand people worked in the mines. The work wasn't bad, but it was dark and potentially dangerous. Nonetheless, I wanted to fulfill my three-year contract.

Chapter 8

A Tempestuous Thursday

I was interested in how the days of the week got their names. In Chinese, Monday was 月, *yui*, named for the moon, the conqueror of darkness, the queen of the night. Mondays, the first working day of the week, could begin quietly. On Tuesdays, you had to work hard; that was the day of fire, 火, *huo*. Wednesday was what the Americans called hump day, like a camel's hump that could store water, 水, *shui*. Thursdays were the most dangerous; in German, it's Donnerstag, the day dedicated to the god of thunder; in Chinese, it's 木, *mu*. Friday was the start of the weekend, where you are physically and mentally free from work; in Chinese, 金, *jin*.

Saturday in German is sonnabend, sunset, it's a day when you can watch the sun set in peace; it's 土, tu, in Chinese. The seventh day of the week is the first day of creation; in Chinese, Sunday is 日, ri. On Sunday, we should praise God, think of life, and leave our memories of the past week behind.

My German was better than that of the other apprentices, so I was working with a German master, Manfred Fischer, who was twenty-seven and well trained in ventilation in the mines, a necessity for miners. The ventilation system was very complex—fresh air had to come in, and stale air had to be pumped out. One Thursday, Manfred and I were checking out a problem with the ventilation system. We tested the fans, pumps, hoses—everything. We crawled down shafts on all fours as if we were James Bonds on a mission, and our hands and knees were bloody. I had trained hard in the military, so I was mentally and physically prepared for the work. But Siegfried, my roommate, who was with us, had been a banker in Korea, and he was having a hard time.

"Hey Master," I asked Manfred, "how far have we gone today?"

"About twelve thousand yards."

We had to constantly wait for Siegfried, who had said he weighed 170, but was more like 220. He found it hard climbing up. And he ate so much garlic that his farts were hard to deal with in the enclosed space. Manfred was too polite to complain about that, though.

I didn't like Siegfried, but I was ashamed of that; I felt that I lacked virtue. *I'm sorry, Siegfried*, I said to myself. But besides being physically weak, he was psychologically weak. He was defensive; he gave up too easily. He was almost like a mollusk.

We all have some knowledge of human nature. When assessing other people, we pay attention to their behavior and try to determine their motives, goals, feelings, and abilities. We shouldn't judge others, but it is natural and essential to do that.

I wanted Siegfried to succeed and reunite with his wife in Berlin, but he had to try harder. I realized he was not fit for work underground; he needed a job above ground. I was afraid for his safety in the mines.

Before the bus took us home, we ate sausage and drank beer in the canteen. Sausage made me happy, and beer is a great way to wash the coal dust out of your mouth.

Chapter 9

Piecework

Our master told us how coal had formed. Millions of years ago, ferns and other growing things fell to the ground and were compacted with later growth, water from floods, and sand, and they formed seams of coal—carbonized vegetation. In the Ruhr region, there are about a hundred of these seams, which formed over millions of years. As the earth's crust shifted, these seams slid over each other.

Coal came to be known as "black diamonds" because it was very valuable, but it had to be mined, that is, extracted from the ground. The seams of coal are not all the same thickness—they vary from a few inches to several yards.

In mining, two parallel tunnels will be bored on either side of a coalface, which can be a hundred yards long. The coal is freed by the cutting action of a machine called a hobel, and it is loaded on conveyor belts to be taken out and transported to the surface. The cavities in the coalface created by this process have to be braced and supported so the coalface doesn't cave in. To support the resulting cavity necessitated our using wooden pillars, tree trunks, that were set vertically and fixed in place.

But the mine I worked in had only two of these coalfaces; the rest of the mining was done by hand. The incline of the face had to be maintained at fifteen degrees. They were worked by guest workers who used hammers driven by compressors. In my coalface, six

Koreans and two Turks worked under the supervision of a German master. We each worked on ten-yard-long sections of the face and loaded our coal into wagons on tracks like a train.

For my piecework, I would earn about forty marks per day. I tried to calculate how much I could save. For my studies, I would need five hundred marks per month, so that would be eighteen thousand I could earn in three years. I needed to earn more.

I studied German until 10:00 p.m. in spite of my aches and pains from working, and I would wake up at 5:20 a.m. so I wouldn't miss the bus to work or make the driver angry. Two minutes before 6:00 a.m., we entered the main shaft. We had to walk for about half an hour to reach our coalface and take our positions at it so we wouldn't crowd each other. The master turned the air compressor on to power our hammers. Before starting to work, I looked around thoroughly to spot any potential hazards, and I would make suggestions to improve safety. I had not forgotten what I had learned in Korea while training. I made seventy marks my second day of piecework.

Part 3

The Work Life

Chapter 10

Homo Sapiens

It was September. The weather was cool, dark, and moody. Leaves were falling. It was raining, but we saw only older people using umbrellas as we waited for the bus to work.

During the ride to work, we Koreans slept, but the Turks and the Germans never did. We Koreans were sometimes passive; we liked playing cards and complaining about our hard work. But we wanted to earn good money.

One day, the coal seam was hard as granite, tougher than it had been the day before. I realized we needed to blast it with explosives.

"Mr. Boss, the coal seam is very hard; our air hammers are not effective on it. But I have an idea—drill and blast."

"What? That's almost forbidden!"

"But you can see for yourself how hard it is."

The master had a silly look on his face. The district overseer came up, and I decided to try my luck with him.

"Gluck auf, Mr. District Overseer!"

"Gluck auf, Mr. Lee!"

"I have been waiting for you, sir. I have to say that the coal is too hard to work with our pneumatic hammers."

"Let's see."

The district overseer followed me to my place and tried to use a pneumatic hammer on the seam; he had no success. His eyes were sparkling, but his face was black.

"Sir, I suggest we drill holes and blast the coal."

He looked at me calmly as he thought. "Mr. Lee, we'll give it a try."

He went away and came back with a German driller, a Turkish helper, and the German demolition expert. They tried drilling, but even that was hard. The driller said, "Leck me im Arsch!" literally "Lick me in the arse," the bawdy words of a piece Mozart composed (K. 231) that I was familiar with. Germans could be vulgar and ignorant; they could also be very expressive.

It took almost half an hour to drill a hole in the coal. The blaster filled it with explosives. We evacuated the tunnel. The district overseer said, "Mr. Lee, go up and tell them all that they must not enter the seam for the next five minutes." He turned to the team leader. "Herbert, close off the air."

After everyone was evacuated, the explosives expert pressed a lever on a battery, and we heard a loud boom. Coal dust quickly covered our faces.

The district overseer gave me a pinch of snuff, but I didn't like it at all. The master turned on the air again, and we waited for the air to clear before we returned to the coalface. I could not understand how such a small amount of explosives could have such a powerful effect. The seam was broken for about twenty feet.

"All right, Mr. Lee?" asked the district overseer.

"Yes sir! Magnificent!"

He left, and I got back to work.

I helped the master load the coal on the wagon. And at the end of the day, he said with a laugh, "Today, you have earned eighty marks, Mr. Lee, and so have I. A good day, Ja?"

"Yes, thank you, sir."

When we got to the exit, we waited for the others. One said to my master, "Hi, Herbert, you old prune! How are you?"

"Shit! Well! How are you, you old ass?"

"Good, good. You're coming to the stadium?"

"Sure. I'll take the trumpet with. One more victory and Bochum's Soccer Team will be Bundesliga." He was referring to the German Soccer League.

We waited in line to take showers. Herbert came up with a bottle of beer for me and asked, "Do you have a wife?"

"Yes."

"Mine was killed in a car accident. Do you have any children?"

"No, not yet."

"I have three. I really do not know how to raise them all by myself.

"I'm sorry. What happened with the car accident?"

"She was not at fault. The other man was crazy."

I understood why he seemed depressed. We drank beer and ate sausages in the canteen.

On the bus back, I fell asleep. It had been a very successful day because I had produced a lot of coal. I hoped to continue earning more.

In the evening, I studied German, but it was going slowly for me. I'd listen to TV for unfamiliar words and look them up, and I got to the point that I could understand what was being broadcast, but only with great labor.

Siegfried interrupted my studying. "Assistant interpreter Park said that the district overseer gave you not eighty but a hundred marks today, and he praised you. Today, I earned only thirty-seven marks. I used to be a white-collar worker. I don't like working in the mines. Wahnsinnig!" That meant "insane." He was angry. I tried to ignore him because he was being rude. He was a married man with a child and should have behaved better than that. He finally left the room.

I watched a program on abortion, which was legal in Germany then only if the woman's life was in danger or the fetus was deformed. I learned that some women went to the Netherlands for abortions. The Netherlands was the only European country where abortions were fully legal. That was the case in Korea too.

I woke the next day to birds singing. The weather looked better.

I stretched my body vigorously. My shoulders hurt a little, but otherwise, everything was fine.

During the next three weeks, we blasted more coal, and I was earning a surprising one hundred marks every day. One day, I earned 120 marks. My bank account was getting bigger. On one Friday afternoon, I met the vice director, who invited me to a beer party. At first, I hesitated, but my district overseer gave me a beer and said, "Come on, Lee."

The old man who kept the washrooms clean prepared sausages for us, the thick German sausages I preferred. Sausage and beer tasted wonderful after work. I drank my beer quickly. I wanted more, but I said nothing.

The vice director said, "You can drink as much as you want. The district overseer brought enough. He has made his production goals because you have worked surprisingly well. Thank you, Mr. Lee. Gluck auf!"

We raised our bottles and clinked them.

It was almost time for me to take the bus back, but the district overseer said, "Mr. Lee, do not worry. We can drive my car. I live in Bochum-Gerthe too."

That meant I could keep drinking and eating.

The vice director said, "Mr. Lee, come tomorrow morning at six. We have a special team for the weekend work under district overseer Neumann. Hey Neumann, tell him where to wait for you tomorrow."

Working on Saturday was very rewarding; the wages were 25 percent more then, but few were given this chance.

"Thank you, Vice Director!" I was very pleased.

I waited for the district overseer. When he came, he told the doorman, "Gluck auf. Please give him the fare."

"Yes, Mr. District Overseer. What is your worker number?"

I did not understand initially that he meant me.

"Mr. Lee, tell him your worker number please."

"Oh. Twelve ninety-one."

"Very good. Here are two marks forty pfennigs. Sign here please."

The district overseer drove a Mercedes-Benz 200 Diesel, which could go faster than a hundred miles per hour. It took only ten minutes to get home. When we arrived, the district overseer said, "Give me the two forty, Mr. Lee."

I did not understand why he wanted 2.40 marks.

"Mr. Lee, you did get two forty for your fare, didn't you?"

"Oh! The fare." I was horrified. A Korean boss would have driven me home for no charge at all, but this was Germany. I gave him the money.

Germans were very confident, while Koreans tended to be passive and reserved. Everything in Korea was affected by Confucianism. I wondered why the director would make our relationship sour for so little money.

Chapter 11

A Disgusting Event

I became known as the best Korean miner at work, and I worked every Saturday. The vice director invited me to his house several times, and my overseers did the same.

My friend Hans Mueller lived with his elderly mother, who worked at a department store, and his wife. He was the only academic in the family. His wife was an elementary school teacher, and they had two sons, seven and five. He was a very loving man.

One Saturday in November after work, I was drinking beer in the washroom. Muller dropped me off at home. When I went into the home, five Koreans blocked my way. The two I knew, but other are strange. A taller man grabbed my shirt collar and shook me, but he was not particularly strong, so I stood firm and secure. He looked at me in consternation and then looked at the others, but no one made a move to help him.

The tall weakling said, "Are you our enemy or what? You're earning so much. Where did you come from just now?"

"From work," I answered.

"Work? Did you work alone?"

"No, not alone, but with many others."

"With many? You're the only one here who works on Saturdays. You're our enemy!"

"No. You are all my friends. We work in Germany to make money. Saturday work is not harmful to our fraternity. Between us there is no animosity." I shook off the grip of the tall man and left. Two others tried to stop me, but I brushed past them. I walked into my room and kissed Melanie's picture.

"Is that your girl? Very beautiful and sexy," the weakling, who had followed me, said. He grabbed the picture and threw it to the floor. My eyes flashed with fire. Three of them attacked me.

One of my attackers was Yun. He had been the secretary for a member of parliament from a province who had lost his mandate in the last election. "You pig! Why do you deserve such money? Do you want to be beaten?"

He tried to punch me, but I had practiced judo. I grabbed his wrist and force him to the ground. I attacked the third, who did no better than Yun. The others fled my room. I stood on the two on the ground. "Why did you attack me?"

"Oh! You're hurting me! Let me up!"

"Tell me why you attacked me!"

Both only groaned. I kicked them out of my room. What a disgusting tale.

The next Monday, I was working on the top coalface, where the air was clear and cool. That day, I managed to mine more than sixteen yards, the unit of measurement in the mine. The master told me, "Mr. Lee, I cannot credit you for sixteen, only for ten. I'm sorry. Gluck auf, Mr. Lee."

I wondered why he stole six tons from me. I wanted to find out, so later, I asked the district overseer. He said, "Mr. Lee, you worked very hard today, but sixteen yards is just too much. We can pay eighty marks a day at the most. We pay four and a half marks per yard. I suggest you cut back your production. Do not tell anyone about this conversation."

I realized what he was saying. If I produced that much every day, it would make the other workers look bad. It was not worth arguing about; I did not want to shame the other workers. I started meeting my quotas by noon, and I left early.

On Friday, the vice director invited me again to a beer party after work.

Again, I was highly praised, but I had a bad feeling. He told me he would take me to the mine the next day. I did not mind working on Saturday. That was normal in Korea, but corruption was normal there too; the political system was bad. The state came first; people and their rights came after that. President John F. Kennedy's words "Ask not what your country can do for you; ask what you can do for your country," was not the ethic in Korea.

On Saturday, I worked with the vice director and two German colleagues to open a new coalface. The vice director worked diligently, and he was always willing to help others. He was a very good, confident, and popular superior who lived the French motto, *Noblesse oblige.*

I worked hard that day; my performance was the best of our group, but the vice director paid the Germans seventy marks while he paid me only sixty. He said, "Mr. Lee, you have worked well as usual, but I have only two hundred marks to distribute. I will make up the difference to you another day, okay?"

I agreed. I had no choice. I wanted to keep on working so I could study later.

The next Monday, I solved a problem with a coal bucket that had destroyed some pillars, and I made things right. I had a good reputation by that time for putting everything in order. I got to work on the coal, and I progressed sixteen yards. I earned eighty marks, and I earned another twenty for my work on the pillars.

I heard some Koreans talking.

"Everything is really shit today!" said Kim, who had a big vegetable business in Pusan.

"Why?" asked Hah, a teacher who taught students the Korean SAT.

"My air hose didn't work, and my axe was dull."

"Didn't you sharpen it this morning?"

"Someone stole my axe. This was the only one I could find. It's too old to sharpen."

"My day was shit too," said Rhee, an officer in the ministry of promotion and technology. "My seam had too many stones."

I listened; I didn't say anything as we took showers though they looked at me. I wondered how long I could keep up my work. I thought about marriage, children, and so on. I would have to send Melanie about eight hundred marks every month if she studied at Oxford.

I continued to study German, but I was making little progress. I still could not understand all the news on TV or read the papers easily, even the tabloids. I thought about simply trying to rely on memorization; that was how I had gotten into university. I fell asleep, thinking I would begin my memorization the next day.

The door to my room burst open. "You pig! We'll kill you, you piece of shit!"

A few people surrounded my bed. I stood on it. I was just in my pajamas, but I was ready to defend myself. Shin attacked me first. I kicked him into the corner. Another attacked me and defended himself well. I ran into the corridor to have more room to fight them. Three of them were not joining in the fight, so I could face the fourth of my attackers alone. His attack technique was a special form of tae kwon do called *ulzi*. But I knew ulzi—I could fight offensively and defensively using that technique to counter the opponent. As he approached me to attack, I just stood still. He tried a kick to my face and had not regained his balance before I threw him over to the ground. He could not get up; he had a big bump on his head. The others were gone in a flash; their legs were shaking.

At the end of the fight, people shouted hurrah and gave me words of encouragement. I returned to my room and cleaned up. The fight had been so stupid. It took me some time to fall asleep.

Most Koreans are good people who love their neighbors and take care of others in need, but others have different characters; they can be from closed social environments and be rigid in life and thought and be jealous of others. It is very sad.

Chapter 12

King of the Coal Hewers

I continued to work hard during the week and on Saturdays and every other Sunday. My monthly earnings never dropped below 2,000 marks, and they once reached 2,200. Every month, I saved 1,800, and I soon had 10,000 in the bank. At that rate, I would have 20,000 marks saved by the end of the year. To achieve that, I worked more and more.

But I often drove myself too hard. I would wake up dead tired. I got worse; I was always thirsty but never hungry. My arms and legs felt weak. I just wanted to lie still. That was the first time I had felt like that. I admitted to myself that my physical and spiritual strength were at their end. I urgently needed to get better.

One Monday, I applied for my annual leave. The vice director asked the district overseer, who asked the master, and he told me they could not do without me. But he noticed my poor health.

"Mr. Lee," he said, "I advise you to go to the doctor and get a medical certificate."

I knew that the doctor was under company pressure not to let too many Koreans receive sickness certificates, but I went anyway. He diagnosed me with the flu and gave me some medicine, which wasn't as common in Germany as it was in Korea.

On Tuesday morning, I delivered my sickness certificate to the vice director, who saw how sick I looked and said, "Yes, Mr. Lee, I hope you have a speedy recovery! We'll see you in a week. Gluck auf."

"But, Mr. Vice Directory. I prefer to take a holiday."

"Then do that. I will tell the office that everything is okay."

"Thank you, Mr. Lord."

I got twelve days' leave, as well as a week off work—I could rest a total of eighteen days. I spent the first three days in bed, and I ate some bread and sausage. The food was not fresh, but I had no strength to shop. I could barely think, speak, open my eyes, go to the toilet, or even breathe.

On Saturday morning, I tried to walk, but I immediately became dizzy. I ate a piece of bread that was hard, and I had to use the toilet frequently. I finally got the strength to make some oxtail soup and rice and forced myself to eat. I thought of my dear mother, who always took care of me when I was sick. Ah, I missed her very much!

I felt no emotion when I looked at Melanie's picture. I fell asleep and dreamed that my mother was taking care of me. She held my hands and prayed.

Lala visited me when I was sick, but I was delirious. "Mama, help me please," I said. "Mom, hold my hands."

"Yes, my darling. I'll hold your hand. What do you need?" came the answer, but I knew it was not my mother speaking. "You're sweating so much! Oh, my sweetheart! What's wrong with you? Wake up. I'm here. Lala is with you."

My lover, Dusseldorf, the Rhine Hotel, the Mercedes-Benz— thoughts slowly reappeared in my consciousness. I recognized Lala. I remembered we had slept together twice. But I did not know if I loved her.

"What's wrong? You don't look good. Come on. We're going to Dusseldorf."

She hugged me, and she helped me to put on my jacket and trousers. I just let everything happen. She almost carried me to her car. She told the housekeeper, "Look here! Mr. Lee is very sick. I'll take care of him. Call me if you have any problems."

I stayed with Lala for a week and received her loving care. She gave me nourishing food. I was finally able to see clearly enough to stand. We also made love. I felt fit again.

A week later, I told her, "You've done so much for me. I really thank you. Without you, I would probably have died."

"If you need anything, I'm always there for you because I love you."

"I love you too. I love you very much."

I realized I had said that I loved her; I didn't want to make her sad.

"Thank you, my dearest!" she said in rapture because it was the first time she had heard me use the word *love*. Right then, that was how I felt, and it made her happy. Melanie? I did not know at that moment.

Lala asked me to go with her on holiday, and I agreed. She bought tickets to go from Dusseldorf to Hamburg because I wanted to go to the sea. In a compartment to ourselves on the train, we felt like a young couple. In Hamburg, Lala was a good tour guide; it was as if she had been born only for me as my slave, or servant, or loving mother.

We stayed in a hotel in St. Pauli, close to the sea. I saw many seagulls circling the water looking to catch fish. The waves sparkled in the sun. It was a wonderful, romantic scene that moved me deeply.

"Honey, what are you thinking?" Lala asked.

"Check out the beautiful ocean and the sun, which is setting. The story of Moses."

"Yes, I see the path the sun is making," she said and squeezed my arm. Her body excited me. I turned around, hugged her, and kissed her ardently.

"My dearest," she said, "make me even happier. I love you, and I want to have your baby. I will not upset your marriage. I just want to raise your baby."

I wanted to create a baby with Lala as an expression of our love, but that was a sin. Melanie's and my happiness would depend on Lala's will. I wanted to do God's will.

I wanted to go to the theater. The Russian ballet was putting on a performance of *Swan Lake*, which I had always wanted to see. When Lala heard this, she ordered front-row tickets. I loved the ballerinas who looked so gentle and could jump high and move gracefully. Tchaikovsky's music was beautiful. The strings played. The swans danced. I began to dream.

The next day, we saw a play about the Irish in which the hero died in the fight against the oppressors of his country.

We stayed one week in Hamburg, and Giesela and Yoyo met us at the train station. I gave the three women small gifts I had bought secretly in Hamburg. All were very happy, particularly Lala.

We had a party at the hotel for Rhee, a nephew of Yoyo who studied in Cologne. He was impertinent, arrogant, overbearing, and boastful, so I spoke little with him. Yoyo asked me to help him with his study of German.

When Park and Lee came, Rhee's mood got even worse. When he made some insulting remarks, Yoyo and Park rebuked him. He even insulted me after he had drunk too much wine. He shouted, "Who are you? Sister Lala's man? You beggar. You son of a bitch. Nigger miner."

I remained seated quietly and just drank my wine until he stood up and tried to hit me. I grabbed his wrist, pulled him into the next room, and threw him to the floor. I made sure his head didn't hit hard by putting my foot under it first. When I returned to dine, Lala offered me a new glass of wine while Yoyo was shouting at Onion, as she called Rhee, "Onion! Open your eyes! Oh, Onion!"

Lala ran over to them, and Park and Lee followed her, but I quietly drank my wine. I knew he would wake up in a few minutes. He had just fainted.

Lala came in and said, "Honey, on behalf of Yoyo, sorry."

Until then, she had never seen me angry. She looked at me anxiously. The unconscious Onion had made an impression on her. Park and Lee came back in the dining room and gave me scared looks, but I filled their wineglasses and forced myself to say, "Cheers!"

Then after a few more glasses of wine, Mr. Park said, "Joseph, the vice director asked for you to please come back to work though you have some days left for you holiday. This is a request and a command."

Should I cancel my holidays and go back to work? But I had had twelve days off, and I was well rested.

Lala said, "Honey, you should go to work on Monday. Usually in Germany, no one interrupts your holidays, but if the vice director asks, that means there is an important problem."

"Yes, my dear. Brother Park, when will you return to Bochum? I'll be happy to share a ride," I said.

"Tomorrow afternoon about four. Good. We can go together."

"Honey, I'll drive you," Lala said. "Will you stay for dinner?"

"That's even better."

On Sunday night, I went with Lala to Bochum.

She brought enough food to last me a month. I thanked her for that and her love. But I thought of Melanie—*Honey, I'm sorry, but I haven't really betrayed you. I was too sick.*

After the long break, it was hard to go back to work. I got up in the morning, took the bus to work, and labored there. I had to catch up to the others. When the master passed, me, he asked, "Mr. Lee, do you have your four yards about finished?"

"Yes sir, Master."

"Well, wonderful. Carry on."

I worked diligently.

The vice director called me, the master, and the district overseer together.

"We set up a special working group for this coalface," he said. "We need to change the work plan. Lee, you have to work two shifts. We need thirty yards a day; if necessary, ask the district overseer and the master to help you, Joseph Lee, the king of the coal hewers."

So I was the king of the coal hewers, but I was working sixteen hours per day. However, I was earning 120 marks per day. I told the district overseer, "Tomorrow, I will do twenty-four yards, but I might have to work until five in the afternoon."

"Well, you do that."

But by five in the afternoon, there would be no bus to take me back. I told the vice director about that, and he called Fritz. "Hey, Fritz! Do you still have that old car? ... Yes? ... Well, send it over immediately."

I went to the personnel office and got the keys for a '60 Volkswagen, which made me very happy. I named her Christina after the mine I was working in of course.

Insurance for Christina cost me twenty-five marks for six months, but I didn't mind paying that at all. Even though the first time I tried to start her up, her battery died. I had to get it charged.

Chapter 13

Improving My German

For laborers, weekends are often boring. On weekends, Koreans in Germany usually slept until noon and then went to movies or played cards. In the evenings, they watched TV until it went off the air. Some Koreans played the lottery, but I never knew anyone who had won at that.

My weekends went from Saturday afternoon to Sunday evening, and I studied German during that time. I needed knowledge of the language to fulfill my dreams. I needed to expand my everyday German vocabulary and ability to speak it, which I did by going to pubs, parks, churches, and the theater.

I was invited to the home of a Protestant pastor, and I enjoyed speaking German with his children. My superiors at the mine frequently invited me to their homes. But I still struggled with the language. I struggled with what I heard on TV, and when I read German, I had to look up so many words, and I struggled to understand the articles I read in the newspapers.

I decided to find a tutor for the weekends, and after asking many people, I found one through Cho, a Korean who had played volleyball on the Korean national team. Cho coached a team at a college in Bochum. Volleyball wasn't that popular in Germany, but the '72 Olympics in Munich had sparked some interest in the sport.

Cho introduced me to Joseph Mueller, a law student at Ruhr

University in Bochum. He tutored me for only two months, but I learned a lot from him—the dative and accusative cases and which prepositions go with them, the use of adverbs, and so on. He stressed the importance of pronunciation, and he helped me very much in terms of my pronunciation.

He also taught me how to write essays—define terms, present the problem in general, explain the content, organize the information logically, and so on. I had learned these principles at university, but to formulate my thoughts in German was not easy. I realized how much depended on a large vocabulary as well as understanding the rules of grammar. German readers and listeners quickly lose their interest if they are reading or hearing anything that is grammatically incorrect. You don't pay a fine for bad grammar as you would for ignoring a red light as you're driving, but you do lose the interest of others. I learned to think about what I said before I said it, and I learned it was possible to avoid mistakes.

I was very grateful to Mueller for his efforts and commitment to teaching me High German, but my language ability was still too low, so I continued my efforts to memorize as much as I could. Memorization was decried in Korea as a poor method of learning, but it was the only way for me to get ahead in the language. I think that without a certain amount of memorization, no language learning is possible.

I learned every day by reading books, newspapers, and magazines. My German textbook was written by Hueber Heart: *The German Language—Basic and Intermediate*. Sometimes, I had to read something twenty times, but by then, I understood it completely. I finally learned to somewhat master the German language. Later, I was able to handle my exams, and my ability in the language impressed my superiors at work.

Part 4

The Romantic Life

Chapter 14

A Beautiful Bride Uses a
Sink as a Chamber Pot

I worked at the mines with Gill Billy, a twenty-five-year-old pharmacist, the only son of a famous physician in Seoul. For four generations, there had only been one son in the family, and that was considered very negative in Korea; the family's survival depended on sons. Because Gill was rather feeble, he did not work underground. He called me his brother because I had once helped him out of a dangerous situation.

One Sunday in October, I was walking in the dormitory yard and memorizing German words. I passed by barracks V and heard noises; some of the workers were playing a Korean card game. I went inside to see what was going on. Billy was dealing, and he was winning a lot of money. The other players were nervous. They finally ended up losing four hundred marks to him.

After a while, the strongest of them said, "Hey, Billy, I've lost everything. How can I last until next payday? Please give me back a hundred marks."

"Me too," both the other players said.

"What are you talking about? Are you crazy? No. I have won it fair and square."

"But consider our situation."

"No, I won't!"

One of them suddenly attacked Billy, who threw him into a corner, but another shoved Billy into the wall, knocking him unconscious. The three quickly left the room. But someone else grabbed Billy and threw him violently against the wall. He bounced on his head and lay there.

Billy's face was white as snow, and his lips were blue. I quickly started mouth-to-mouth respiration on him and kept it up for fifteen minutes. It was very difficult. He suddenly started coughing up foam. After a while, he calmed down, and his face returned to normal. I made tea for him. After that, he started calling me brother because I had saved his life.

He was going to get married, and he wanted me to be his best man. It was the first wedding among the Koreans in Bochum. His fiancée, Elisabeth Bae, or Elza for short, worked as a nurse. She was twenty-six, and she came from Billy's area in Korea; their families knew each other. She was helping to support her family back home.

The ceremony took place in an auditorium at the hospital. The bride was very beautiful; she was also taller than Billy, who had to wear shoes with two-inch heels to match her height. A girlfriend of the bride played the wedding march on the piano, and the bridesmaid was a good girlfriend; the three had been friends since high school.

The wedding ceremony proceeded solemnly until three men crashed through the door. One yelled, "Stop! Stop! She's my wife! This marriage is invalid!"

I was very furious and stepped in front of the couple. "Anyone who tries to stop this is a dead man!" I yelled.

His two companions ran forward and attacked me, and they obviously knew karate. I threw one to the ground, but it took me a while to kick drop the other. I took a deep breath, jumped up, and again took a fighting stance. One tried to kick my chin, but I ducked and grabbed his ankle and kicked him in his weakest spot. He cried out and fell down. The attackers were no longer so self-assured. They were taken out of the auditorium by three of the groom's friends, who made them sit under a tree. I went over to them and asked, "Who are you? Why did you do that?"

They were silent.

I grabbed the group's leader and threw him into the air. He landed with a thump.

"You have five seconds to get out of here before the bride sees you! One, two, three, four ..." I counted.

They vanished, and the rest of us went to a great restaurant to celebrate the wedding.

A year later, Elza bore a son.

She told me her story. She and her two friends had come to Germany in 1965, when they were seventeen, to attend a vocational school with a nursing program in Bonn. They lived in a hostel for student nurses in Bonn. She slept in a room with eight other students in a room on the second floor; the toilet was on the ground floor.

One of her friends who was scared to go downstairs at night would use the sink in the room as a toilet, and Elza decided to do that one night. She sat on the sink and broke it. Water gushed out and soaked Elza and the whole room. The water leaked down to the floor below; that was where older nurses lived. A fireman came and turned off the water.

The next morning, the cause of the flood came to light. All three girls transferred to a nursing school in Osnabruck.

How Billy met Elza in Osnabruck is a very funny story as well. He was small, weak, and not handsome, but he was very clever. In Korea, he was enrolled at the university but had to stop due to an illness. The cause of his illness was a mystery; even his father, a university-educated doctor and specialist in Chinese medicine, could not determine its cause. Just as Elza was leaving for Germany, Billy went into the hospital.

When his health improved, he finished his studies and served his time in the military. After his time in the military was finished, he told his father that he wanted to go to Germany to earn money; he had not been able to obtain a job in his profession.

He went to Germany, and he started visiting cities there where Korean women were studying and working, including West Berlin, Munich, and Stuttgart. He wanted to go to the United States, and he knew that many Korean nurses in Germany later moved to the United States. He hoped to marry such a nurse and move with her to the United States.

On a visit to Osnabruck, he met Elza, whom he had known since childhood. She was very happy to see him again, and he was very impressed with the adult Elza. One thing led to another, and they decided to marry.

But who were the Koreans who had disturbed the wedding? One was a Korean engineer who worked in Nuremberg; he had visited a relative in the nurses' home, saw Elza, and fell in love with her immediately. He started visiting her frequently and brought presents each time, but she thought she was too young for marriage. In particular, she did not want to return to Korea.

After she graduated, she told no one in her family where she had gone. The engineer, however, convinced the staff at the school to give him her address; he said he wanted to visit her. That was how he had found out she was in Osnabruck, and he charged into the wedding.

There was another man who was interested in Elza; he worked in a dairy factory in Essen and dreamed about opening a dairy in Korea; he logically wanted to name it after Louis Pasteur—Pasteur-Yang. He was thirty-one and therefore wanted to get married as soon as possible. Korean men are usually married by age twenty-nine, and Korean women are usually married by age twenty-five.

He was a Catholic and had found a Korean Catholic Community in Essen. The Korean Catholic Association in Essen opens year-end party of each year, and at that meeting, he fell in love at first sight he saw Elza.

The festival ended late, so she had to spend the night in a hotel. Pasteur followed her there and knocked on her door.

"Who's there?" she asked.

"I'm the president of the Catholic Association in Essen. I would like to talk to you about a church matter. May I come in?"

"Could you please come back tomorrow? It's after midnight."

"I would like to, but I have a prayer service tomorrow morning. Do you have just a few minutes?"

Elza thought he was a gentlemen because he was a good Catholic. But as soon as she opened the door, he lunged at her like a tiger. He ripped off her skirt and tugged at her bra.

Elza had been in a similar situation with the engineer and knew how to handle it. She looked at him lovingly and said, "Wait! Let me take a shower first."

This confused the Catholic so much that he let go of her.

"Do you want to take a shower first?" she asked him.

He was congratulating himself for having found a woman who was so cleanly. "You shower first," he said.

"Thank you, sweetheart. I'll be fast," she said while looking at him sweetly.

She went in and took a shower. She came out with a towel around just her lower body, and that excited Pasteur. She said coquettishly, "Hurry up! I'll wait for you."

Pasteur rushed to the bathroom, undressed, and got under the shower, but in his haste, he turned on just the hot water and burned himself before he could turn off the faucet. His manhood was dangling, and it took him a while to get it into its correct position.

He exited the bathroom and did not see Elza. He thought she was hiding. "Elza, where are you?" No answer.

Elza had gleefully heard his screams when he was under the hot water. She got dressed, left the room, and locked it from the outside.

Pasteur was burned, and he could not sleep because of the pain and his memories of Elza's beautiful body.

Elza and Billy had two more sons, and three years later, her family visited Seoul. Billy's parents threw a big party for Elza's family and gave Elza's parents a big shop in Seoul.

Chapter 15

Korea's First Gold at the Olympics—1972 Munich

I got a two-week holiday to help the Korean team at the Olympics in Munich in 1972; the Korean embassy in Bonn had asked me to do that. I made calls and sent papers, but mostly, I was an interpreter. That was the Olympics at which terrorists killed members of the Israeli team; in spite of the tragedy, the games went on.

One day, I received a call from the police; I had to talk to a Korean who had been arrested. The Korean consul was not available, so they called me.

When I walked into the police station, policeman pointed his gun at me. "Hands high! Turn around. Lean against the wall! Legs wide!"

I was shocked, but I did what he said. He asked me who I was and what I wanted. He had not been told I was coming, and he perhaps mistook me for a terrorist because of my long hair; I didn't want to spend money on barbers. I did not look like a Korean diplomat. When I explained my situation in detail, he laughed and took me to the arrested Korean, who turned out to be someone I knew. His name was Bergstone; he lived in the same place I did.

"Brother Lee, help me please!"

"What's going on, Mr. Bergstone?"

"I sold some tickets to make money."

"You are a scalper?"

"That's right. Mr. Lee, help me. I'll give you a thousand marks."

"The police say you have to leave the country in forty-eight hours."

"Mr. Lee, I will not. Please help me. I'll give you two thousand. Please!"

"No. I cannot accept money from you. We can try to change the penalty to a fine so you don't have to leave the country."

"How much will the fine be?"

"I do not know."

He thought for a while. "I'll do what you say. I want out of here!"

I spoke with the policeman about changing the legal charge and fining Bergstone rather than taking him to court. He said that might take a week. In the meantime, they would keep him in his cell. I asked about bailing him out, and the policeman said that would be 3,000 marks. Bergstone had only 1,800, so I arranged to pay the additional 1,200.

Bergstone later paid me back the 1,200 marks and offered me an additional 1,000 as a gift, but I refused.

Korea has not won a gold medal in the Olympic history. However, as the chief of Police said: This Olympics was disgraceful at the Munich Olympic Games, but Korea won his first gold medal by Mr. Bergstone.

Chapter 16

The Poker Champion Presbyter Baeg

Almost all the Korean migrant workers in Germany were intellectuals, and they worked hard; industriousness is among the most important virtues in the Confucian tradition. In China, Confucius was as important as Aristotle was in Europe. His students wrote out his ideals in the book Luen Yue, (論語, *The Talks*). Many of Korea's customs derive from this book. Master Confucius taught,

> The superior man never eats so much that he is eating to excess; in his house, he does not demand convenience; he is diligent and careful when working in his statements; he associates with those who follow the right path and thereby helping from his shirt. From such a man can say that he has a sense of learning actually, Koreans depart from these rules at times when it comes to singing, dancing, and playing cards—gambling. I do not know exactly when or where it began, but some Koreans at work gambled heavily and would lose so much that they had no money to send home to their families. Every night, I heard the cries of the losers and the happy shouts of the winners. Some, especially those who worked the early shift, complained about the noise. But some of the

gamblers played all the time and even throughout the weekends without a break.

The Protestant presbyter Baeg was a very devout and industrious man. He had been an elder in a Methodist church in Korea. He was thirty-four and had been a primary school teacher. He went every Sunday to the evangelical church in Bochum-Gerthe, and the local pastor liked him so much that he invited him to dinner. Presbyter Baeg tried to get the atheists among us go to church and actually converted four of them.

His German was not that good, so if he was invited somewhere or wanted to buy a gift for his wife back home or his pastor, he asked me to come along. If I had time, I would do so because he was a quiet, loyal, and friendly person. And it was also a good time for me to practice my German.

After some of the successful poker players had won as much as they could from other gamblers, they looked for new victims, and among them was Baeg. They let him win at first to build up his interest in gambling. He learned the rules of the game quickly. As his winnings grew, so did his interest in gambling.

Ko, the leader of the players, was a former manager of a casino in Pusan. He was thirty-seven, and he was sixth degree in tae kwon do. The presbyter played well enough that he quickly won eight hundred marks; he gave them to me for safekeeping, though initially, I did not know why.

The betting became heavier because the gamblers wanted to make up for their losses, but Baeg kept winning and winning. One day, he gave me ten thousand marks to send to his family in Korea. That was much more than he was earning at work. I asked him about it, and he told me about his gambling success. The other gamblers were threatening him. He no longer wanted to play, but the others forced him to play because they wanted to win their money back. Nonetheless, he always won because he prayed to God before every game.

The police heard about the gambling, and one Saturday night, they raided the place and jailed eight players. Baeg had to pay a ten-thousand-mark fine. Thus ended the gambling career of presbyter Baeg, the master poker player.

Chapter 17

Under an Assumed Name

The posting of Koreans to foreign work positions began in the 1960s. Koreans could work abroad only once; maybe that was to give others a chance. But some workers returned; they found ways to get around the rules.

Lee, whom I worked with, was thirty-five, well educated, and the father of three. He was tall and handsome. I knew him only slightly, but when he got into a big problem later, he asked me for help, and so I learned his history.

He had worked from 1965 to 1968 in Germany. But while he was away from home, his wife met someone else and spent all the money he had sent to her from Germany. His children were living with his brother in Korea. In Korea, it is customary for the wife of the eldest son to take care of his parents, but his wife did not take care of them or her children. When Lee got back, the family was broken apart and all his money was gone. Lee was heartbroken. He decided to go back to work in Germany using his brother's name. That time, he planned to send his money back to his brother.

In Lee's home in Germany were three German and Turkish women who cleaned houses. Edith Grosser was one of those three; she was thirty-three, widowed, and childless. Her parents lived in East Germany. She fell in love with Lee, who was lonely and sad, but he was also conservative and passive.

Edith approached him slowly and carefully; their love was pure for a year and a half, but one day, she invited him into her room. Their love grew and became passionate; they were adults, and they were in love.

Six months before Lee was to return to Korea, Edith became pregnant. She hoped, of course, that Lee would stay with her and the baby. But Lee was concerned about his children in Korea and the fact that he was in Germany using his brother's name. He needed help, and he came to me.

I listened attentively and realized that to solve his two problems, he had to return to Korea to sort the matter out. Edith was worried he would not return if he went, and that was another problem. But if he married her, he would not need a visa to come back.

I told Edith I wasn't a lawyer, but I wanted her to gain confidence in the plan. I told her, "Dear Edith, do not worry. When Lee goes to Korea, he will be your husband, I swear to you. But he needs to solve a problem in Korea."

"What problem?" She didn't know about the problem with his name.

"His real name is Lee Lyun. Lee Lyon is the name of his brother." The difference between their names was the difference between an *o* and a *u*.

I explained the matter to her.

"Is his wife still alive? I can get help to support his three children here, I promise you."

"Thank you, dear. First, we go to a lawyer and let him certify that you are going to have a baby with him. Lee will be obligated to support the child until age eighteen no matter where he is."

"Joseph, you're a wonderful troubleshooter! Thank you. I will do what you told me. Let's go at once."

"Edith, Lee is an honest man. He keeps his promises. Believe him. Trust between a husband and wife is very important."

"Yes, Joseph. Thank you."

I told Lee to ask his brother to send his passport by express mail. When we took it to the lawyer, the lawyer signed the necessary papers. He did not recognize the difference between Lyon and Lyun.

Lee flew to Korea, and three months later, Edith gave birth to a son with black eyes, but his other features were Western. Edith longed for Lee when she looked at their baby. Without talking with Lee, she named her son Joseph, after me.

Lee had troubles getting a visa to return; that took six months. I had to help him out by writing many letters, but his brother's lawyer helped too.

One day, Edith visited me with her baby wrapped on her back in the Korean fashion. "I once saw on TV that Korean mothers carry their babies on their backs. I am now a Korean mother, so I have my child wear on my back, right?" Then she cried.

But not long after that, she told me Lee would be arriving in Germany in five weeks. "Thank you!" she said. She cried again just like a Korean mother. But little Joseph showed his most beautiful smile.

Chapter 18

Three Encounters with
the Angel of Death

I once heard that those who survive danger three times will receive much money, honor, and power in life. Nonetheless, I was careful to avoid accidents. I needed money to study and achieve a better life, but I didn't want to risk injury or death to do that.

Nonetheless, I did experience three very dangerous situations.

The First Encounter: Lala's Parents

I loved Melanie, so my relationship with Lala was a sin. She gave birth to my son and named him Joseph Junior. However, his family name was Yuh since we were not married, and her father had no son. So she introduced her son as her father's son. She, the mother, became junior Joseph's sister. But I learned all this much later.

One Saturday morning, Lala came to see me, but I was at work. She saw Melanie's photo. Melanie had received a scholarship to study at Oxford. She and I had married. Indeed, she was a great woman and a very worthy wife. Lala was happy for me; she was not jealous or envious of Melanie. She was happy that she had had a son with me. She left a letter for me; I did not know why she had visited me; we had not seen each other for a year.

The next Monday, I got a telegram from the Korean embassy in Bonn; the embassy wanted me to take part in a ceremony at which two Korean ministers would be present. President Park had awarded me a medal because I had helped many Koreans with their problems in Germany.

Many Koreans attended the even—students, businesspeople, professors, and others. As an honor, I sat between the prime minister and other minister, the two officials who were closest to President Park. We feasted on Korean food and liquor that had been flown in from Korea.

As the ambassador presented medals to me and a nurse, the prime minister looked at me strangely, but I did not know why. The event ended at half past ten, and as I was leaving, the ambassador told me that the prime minister wanted to talk to me. He led me to his office, where the prime minister was with a woman in a beautiful, traditional Korean robe.

"Good evening, Mr. Lee," said the prime minister. "I am the father of Lala, and this is her mother. I congratulate you on the medal President Park has given you, a great honor."

I was shocked. *Lala's father and mother!*

Lala's mother was furious with me. "You must take responsibility for Lala and your son! You must divorce your wife in Oxford and marry Lala, do you understand?" Her voice was dripping with malice and poison. "Even though you are small, you seem bright, and you speak good German. The president thinks you are worthy of a medal, but you are actually a very greedy person!"

The prime minister spoke. "No, Mother. You've heard what Lala said. Calm down. Mr. Lee, I want to talk to you about Junior. He is now my son. Is that a problem for you? You have to waive your paternal rights or you'll get into a great deal of difficulty."

"I am very pleased to meet Lala's father and mother," I said. "I heard that you registered Junior as your son. I will give up my parental rights."

But Lara's mother wanted me as a son-in-law.

"Thank you very much, Mr. Lee. I hope you tell Lala that. Mother, let's go. Oh, yes, I have heard that you want to study. Is that true?"

"Yes."

"What do you want a study?"

"Pedagogy—education science."

"Very good. In Korea, there are many with degrees who studied in the United States, but few have degrees from Europe. Earn your doctorate quickly. Our homeland needs you. We are interested in the German school system. When you get your PhD, get in touch with me. Maybe I can help you reform our school system. Goodbye, Mr. Lee. I think you are a good man."

Lala's mother looked back at me three times as they left. I got home at two in the morning and had to sleep before I worked the next day, but I had a severe headache. Lala's mother's voice was still in my mind.

The next day, we finished creating a two-hundred-yard-deep vertical cylinder; ten thousand tons of coal would come out if it every day. It was wet down there, and my shoes were already soaked. The situation was very dangerous since the shaft was vertical, and it was dark. We had to wear safety belts and hold them with one hand; we could use just one hand to work. My head was full of Lala, her mother, and Junior.

And then something happened. Everything went black.

I felt nothing. I saw a man smiling at me. "Who are you? Are you a foreigner? Chinese or Japanese? Hmm. Do you know why you're here?"

"Who are you? Are you Beelzebub or Lucifer? I'm Korean. What happened? I love my wife, and Lala perhaps, and she has a son from me, but not for me, for herself. What do you want with me?"

"I'm the angel of death. All are equal in the grave. I can take you to the kingdom of God, but you're not ready to go. Be careful or I'll have to take you to the underground kingdom," he said and ran away, his words echoing in my mind.

"Joseph, are you okay?"

"Yes, thanks, Mueller."

"You fell unconscious. I'll pull you up. Manfred, help! Wait, Joseph. You won't die."

I was hoisted up. My legs felt quite weak. They pulled me up about a hundred yards.

On Sunday, I was running a high fever. On Monday, the house doctor diagnosed me with overexertion, so I could not go to work.

That night, Lala came to tell me that her father had a favorable opinion of me, but when she saw me sick again, she cried.

The work that week was very hard.

The Second Encounter: Jacob's Ladder

After my first meeting with the angel of death, I did not want to work weekends, but the vice director wanted Mueller and me to repair some of the wood bracing at a coalface that was just below the Ruhr River and was very wet.

We had to drag the wood we needed a long distance; these were like railroad ties—a foot wide, and a foot tall, and seven feet long. We dragged a hundred of them about eighty yards. We had to use them to stabilize the pillars, and it was dangerous and difficult work. We had to cut away some of the coalface in the passage to get the seven-foot-long ties around some corners.

As we were doing that, some of the face shifted and crumbled. I was almost buried in scree. I was flat on the ground and could barely breathe. I could not move my arms. I had lost my helmet with its lamp.

"Mueller! Help me! Mueller! Where are you? I cannot move! Come quickly, please." No one answered. I tried to free myself, but

I could not. *Will I die? No! I love Melanie and Lala as well. I have to earn a PhD. I must live for my homeland and my family!* All my strength was gone. I felt nothing but peace. I thought I was dying.

I dreamed I saw a stairway that led to heaven; God's angels were going up and down it. It was a very beautiful scene. Someone whom I thought was Jesus sat by me and said, "Come on, let's go to eternal life! You want to live forever, right?" He pointed at a tall ladder that led up.

"Yes, thank you." I walked toward the ladder, but the man grabbed me.

"Who are you?"

"I am Joseph Lee from Korea."

"Who? My God! Are you back again? No! I would take Joseph Conrad or Joseph Schindler, but not you! Go back!"

He let go of my arm and left. The angel of death guided me back to life

I woke up and realized I was still buried. I heard someone say, "Joseph, if you want to live, you need to breathe! Just try to breathe deeply! Good! Work carefully. Joseph, this isn't goodbye. Gluck auf!"

I was able to breathe again. My consciousness came back. Mueller was speaking to me.

"Joseph, answer me! This is Mueller!"

I was so relieved. "Mueller!" Tears choked my words.

"All right, Joseph. I'm here."

Mueller and others finally dug me out.

I was in the hospital in Bochum for four weeks. One day, Mueller came to visit and asked, "Joseph, have you seen the angel of death?"

"Yes."

"What did he say?"

"I was supposed to climb a ladder."

"Joseph, that was Jacob's ladder by which one can go to heaven.

When you see him the next time, he will tell you to give him your right hand. Do not. Give him your left foot. Then you won't die. Do not forget that."

"Ha! This is a joke, right?"

"No, Joseph. This is not a joke. Always be careful when he wants something from you. Always do the opposite."

"Yes, Mueller. Thank you."

Mueller was a real lifesaver. He was a fifty-five-year-old widower; his oldest son was a dentist, the second son taught English, and his daughter worked for the foreign ministry in England. I had met his family, and I liked them very much.

After I got out of the hospital, I was not allowed back to work for two weeks. Lala took me to her house in Dusseldorf, where I was introduced as Junior's uncle.

I was happy when my doctor certified that I could work again. I enjoyed working much more than doing nothing. That was true even though what I earned during my disability leave was 50 percent higher than what I would have earned at work.

The Third Encounter: Foot Instead of Hand

One Saturday, seven months before the end of my employment contract, I planned on spending a quiet evening with Lala in Dusseldorf when the vice director called with the news that a coalface had collapsed. I had to return as fast as I could.

I drove Lala's Benz to Bochum and arrived at nine. The vice director left me a note telling me I should meet him at the mine. I put on my work clothes and went quickly to the coalface. The pit was empty except for the vice director and Mueller; both were happy to see me.

"Gluck auf, Mr. Lee. Have you seen Overseer Metzger?"

I knew Metzger. He and I had had a quarrel once. I worked for him one day, but he and the crew left before I did, which was against policy. They should have stayed to help me with my work.

About two hours later, I went up. In the shower room, I drank my beer alone. District Overseer Hans passed and was surprised to see me. "Mr. Lee, why are you here alone? Weren't you working on Overseer Butcher's crew?"

Metzger in English means butcher.

"Yes, but they left," I answered. I explained everything.

"That's a shame he didn't help. He and the rest of the crew have already come up and have left. Mr. Lee, on Monday, I'll tell the vice director about this. Butcher will get a penalty."

He was furious, but I remained calm.

Metzger received a warning and a 10 percent reduction in salary, while the others received a 5 percent reduction in salary. Ever since then, Metzger would try to penalize me about my piecework, but the district overseer and the vice director support me, so I was never cheated by Metzger. Nonetheless, there was tension between Metzger and me, and I did not want to see him.

Overseer Butcher arrived with three men, and the vice director told him, "Overseer Metzger, you and your men and Lee are to put this coalface in order. When you finish, call me and wait for me."

The coalface—this one was called Caroline—had a slope of fifteen degrees and was eighty yards long. The seam was about two yards high. It contained anthracite coal, which is soft and rich, thus its name. You had to caress that coal carefully.

We had to shore up where the coal had fallen from the seam. On our team were technical experts as Butcher was, but they weren't miners. I told Butcher what we should do, and we all had to do it together; when the hand does not know what the foot is doing, everything is difficult.

Despite the difficult work situation, we had shored up two-thirds of the eighty yards. We took a break. Butcher sat close to the seam. I said, "Overseer Metzger, this is very dangerous. Please move away from the seam. It is already pulverized coal. Be careful!"

"Mr. Lee!" he yelled. "I am your overseer. You have no idea of coals or mines. I have studied for four years at the Mining Academy."

He started pounding on the seam, and coal dust fell from the ceiling. I pulled one of our crew away from the area with me, and we went to the top as quickly as we could. When we had gone about twenty yards, we heard something that sounded like rain falling. I could see nothing but dust.

We waited a few minutes before we went back. The seam had dropped off for about sixteen yards. I could not see the butcher. I was sure he was buried in the coal.

I called out to the butcher. No answer. I found his helmet and lamp, and I started digging in the coal dust. I found him and tried to pull him out, but he was big. I couldn't move him. I heard coal starting to fall again. I let go of the overseer. I was buried by the second avalanche.

My legs were free, but not my arms. Some thick stones were pressing into my back. I could breathe, but my mouth was full of coal. I had no idea where the overseer was. Everything around me was quiet; nobody called me. I could not move. Before my eyes appeared Melanie, Lala, and Junior, but that time, I felt nothing. They were so far away. It was a sad feeling.

"Hello! Help!" I shouted. My eyes filled up with tears of anger. *No! This is not worth tears. I have to fight for my life!* I remembered Psalm 23, which Melanie had taught me: "The Lord is my shepherd, I will lack nothing. He makes me lie down in green pastures and leads me beside still water. Even when I walk through a dark valley, I fear no harm, for You are at my side; Your rod and staff give me courage." That reassured me. I remembered Psalm 121: "The Lord protects you. The Lord is your shade; the sun will not harm even at night the moon. The Lord will guard you from all evil."

Just then, I saw the one person I did not want to see. The angel of death.

"Hmm, hmm. Sad. This is the third time This time, I unfortunately need to take you. Alas, my poor boy."

He looked at me calmly, but I did not move. I wanted to argue with him to gain time. "Are you good or evil? Are you Lucifer, the king of evil?"

"No. I am the angel of death. Why do you ask?"

"The doomed spirits are fallen angels that did not keep their heavenly dignity and left heaven. Are you a servant and messenger of Satan?"

"Ha! Why do you think that? Who told you that? He should be punished!"

"I don't know who told me that."

"You're a smart guy."

*Perhaps Mueller was righ*t, I thought. *Perhaps he will ask for my hand.* I wanted my hands to hide behind my back, but I could not move them.

"Give me your right hand," he said.

He reached out to me, and I gave him my left foot.

"You're a smart guy. From whom did you learn to give me your foot rather than your hand?"

"My friend Hans Mueller. He was right. It's beyond belief."

"Mueller? Oh yes. Hans Mueller. He was already three times in my grasp. He is a good man, and you are a nice guy. I am sparing your life. I will take Butcher. You will live ninety-nine years. Gluck auf."

He brushed away some coal so I could breathe again. The angel disappeared with Butcher.

I saw Hans Mueller's face. He held my hand. I fell asleep.

When I awoke, a nice sister was washing me. She reminded me of my mother. She smiled. "You are alive. This time, you have been injured. A rib and wrist are broken, but they are clean breaks. I am Korean. You are my son, and I am washing you today for the second time. Okay, done."

I wanted to thank her, but I was wearing an oxygen mask. She was forty-two and had two sons; I think I would be her oldest.

I stayed six weeks in the hospital and a week at home. Then, I went for treatments for four weeks in the Black Forest. The angel of death had promised me I would live to age ninety-nine. Sometimes, I miss him. Almost. Life is a joy. Life is more than just food and drink, as the Bible teaches. We should not worry about things beyond human control.

I had met the angel of death three times. Death is the opportunity to abandon everything. Will I see him again perhaps when I do die? But it is very romantic to rise from the threshold of death. I will always welcome him.

Part 5

The Tragic Life

Chapter 19

The Shock of a Quick Dismissal

Korean workers had many difficulties in Germany. Many were too weak for the hard work, and many developed health problems, especially stomach pains and bronchitis. Most of them had been white-collar people not used to hard work. They were used to handling pens, not pneumatic hammers. They worked at desks, not narrow places underground. Many were afraid of the work, and given the conditions, it was obvious that some would have accidents.

The house doctor was not able to find the cause of the gastritis the miners suffered from frequently, so he studied their eating habits. He made us cook our food in pots that were not aluminum, and he had us do without the very hot pepper that we used to make kimchee, but nothing worked, and some miners were out of work from one month to three months. The vice director wondered what he could do about that, but I had no answer.

Meanwhile, I had become a master over one shift in the mine. Working with me were five Koreans—a former bank employee who was twenty-eight, a former official in the ministry of finance, a former schoolteacher, and a former secretary for a minister, who were all twenty-nine, and the former director of a business that had failed due to bad checks. All five were intelligent; they all had bachelor's degrees. On our first day together, some of them complained that their work sites were too hard, so I changed them around, but I told them I would change them again. We got to work, and we loaded eight carts.

Then Kim showed me that he had injured his thumb. It was not a bad injury, so I told him to continue working.

"No, I can no longer work. I'm a fellow Korean! How can you treat me this way? This is bullshit!"

"Brother Kim, your finger is not seriously injured. Continue working."

"I cannot. The finger hurts. Sign me out of here. Koreans must help other Koreans. You know that, right?"

"Mr. Kim, I have responsibilities here. If you do not get back to work, I will report you to the vice director. Go to your place, and continue working."

If Kim could not work, the workers above him on the coalface would have to stop too because of the distance between the upper and lower part of the coalface. And we were supposed to produce 120 tons during that shift.

Kim left without my permission. I could not stop him. I had to rearrange the workers.

Kim came back with the overseer.

"Master Lee, what's wrong with Kim?"

"He said he hurt his thumb."

"Show me your thumb, Kim."

The overseer looked at the thumb and said, "That's no problem. Go up and continue working."

"No, I cannot," said Kim.

"Master Lee, did you allow him to leave?"

"No. He went without my permission. I told him several times to continue working."

"Well, Mr. Kim, get back to work or you will have to answer to the disciplinary committee. I'll give you three minutes."

"You have to help me, Lee." said Kim.

"I cannot. You must decide."

"You bastard! I'm leaving!"

"Go, then," the overseer said. "And Mr. Lee, see me later so we can put this incident on record. Gluck auf."

"I will. Gluck auf."

The overseer went away, and we got back to work. We loaded 120 tons on that shift. My crew received eighty marks each, and I received ninety.

The overseer had Kim's insubordination passed on to the disciplinary committee even before I got in touch with him. He informed me that Kim and I should report to the vice director the next morning. I got home at two, ate my dinner, and fell asleep. I had a good dream.

"My favorite," Melanie said, "It is the duty of the flowers to bloom. To bring a baby into the world is my duty. You should not thank me. Kiss me, darling."

Suddenly, a strong wind began to blow and dark clouds covered the sky. It quickly became dark. I hugged her and tried to run with her into the house. A bolt of lightning hit me right in the face. I saw Melanie fly through the air. I could not follow her. A second bolt of lightning hit my face. I still wanted to follow Melanie, but I was again hit.

I opened my eyes. Someone was attacking me. I jumped up and slammed my fist into him. I heard a scream and saw a second attacker. I hit him, and he rolled on the floor.

"What's going on?" I was shocked. I was still on the bed defending myself against any further attacks. I saw someone move in the darkness, and I charged him. Another jumped up and tried to run out the door but fell. The room stank of alcohol and vomit. I kicked an attacker, and I dodged a kick aimed at my jaw that would have knocked out some teeth. After I hit him in the stomach, he leaned forward and fell on his face.

Siegfried turned on the light. The attacker who had fallen at the door was Kim. I picked him up. "Why did you attack me?"

I held him by both arms firmly; he was powerless. He stank of alcohol. I allowed the other attacker to sit on the bed. Mr. Rhee, the speaker of our community, came in and took the two away. It was five in the morning, and I ached where I had been hit.

The next morning, I asked the warden for help taking Kim to the vice director, but Kim was not in his room. Even his friends did not know where he was. Someone finally told us we could find him in the city and gave us an address.

We found Kim at twelve, and the warden called the vice director to clarify the situation. Half an hour later, we were sitting in his office. The disciplinary committee dismissed Kim. This was communicated to the police, and Kim lost his visa. He had to leave Germany within two weeks.

I learned later that my other attacker had been Kim's friend, a university student. I had knocked out two of his teeth and had bloodied his nose. His eyes were swollen shut, and his elbow was broken. He lost the right to charge for the cost of treatment due to the fact the injuries were his own fault. He too had to leave the country. The police in Korea sent a memorandum to me when the two went to court. I did not want them punished more, so I asked the embassy in Bonn for leniency for them.

Some Koreans went home due to the stomach pains they were experiencing; others left because they refused to work; and one was dismissed because he failed to show up for work for three days.

Some of the Korean miners didn't care about the three years; they didn't take it seriously. But they should have been thinking about their futures.

Chapter 20

Misfortune

Accidents happen every minute of every day in factories, offices, shops, mines, and at sea. Everywhere. Work can be very stressful, and it can lead to accidents and death when the working conditions are hard, dangerous, dirty, and low-paid. We humans can only work hard and hope to achieve our dreams and goals. But we all face death.

Death is sad, but because it is our destiny, we have to face it with seriousness and dignity. Regardless, the death of a twenty-nine-year-old is incomprehensible. Mr. Hah's death was especially painful for me because he was a friend of mine; he and I had forged plans to study together.

He had been a civil servant in the Ministry of Internal Affairs and secretary to a minister. He had lost his job when his boss stole money and blamed it on him. Hah had married three months before going to Germany, and his wife planned to work as a nurse's assistant to support him when he went to university.

One Friday, I was working with Mueller. We were operating a coal plow. Hah was working with a twenty-one-year-old mechanic who had little experience with the machine, which was dangerous. Hah had even less knowledge of the device. Under such circumstances, an accident was inevitable. Korean miners received training, but not as much as German miners did.

Mueller and I were taking a break when the mechanic ran up. "Accident!"

Mueller and I raced back with the worker. We saw Hah's lifeless body. His neck and jaw had been crushed by the machine. I could not magine how that could have happened. Blood was still running out of his neck.

His death was a major shock to the other Koreans. Up to that point, no one had been killed. We had seen training films about the dangers of coal mining, but we did not worry about becoming victims ourselves—death was far away from our thoughts. But Hah's death was reality. All the Koreans felt as if they had died with him.

A year later, his wife came to Germany and found work at a hospital in Essen. One weekend, she visited me. She was beautiful. She brought her son along, and he looked like his father. I learned later that she married a German, who adopted her son. I will never forget Hah.

Chapter 21

A Silly Suicide

After Joseph Mueller, my English tutor, moved away, I had to learn German on my own, and I was successful. People told me that I spoke German better than other Koreans did. Other Koreans at the mine would come to me with their problems, small and large, for help because of my good German skills; I became known to the Koreans as a resourceful man.

I was not a lawyer and will not likely be, Santa Maria, but some Koreans asked me at times for legal help. I would refer them to a law firm in the city center, but that was expensive.

One day, a young Korean from another German city visited me. His family name was Choi, and he needed a troubleshooter—me. He had a degree from a private university and came from a middle-class family. Choi needed a lawyer to get back fifteen thousand marks he had sent to his girlfriend, Isabel, who studied at the same university where he had studied. They graduated at the same time, but Choi was three years older than she was because he had served in the military for that time.

When he went to Germany, she attended training to become a nurse's assistant. They were planning on marrying. In fact, she came eight months after he did to Germany and found work at a hospital in Monchengladbach.

Choi had repeatedly visited her and given her his entire salary so she could save it. In Korea, wives normally manage the money. She lived in a room next to the hospital rather than in the nurses' quarters; men were not allowed in the nurses' quarters, and he wanted to stay with her when he visited her. When he visited her one day, he met Udo, a young German in her room, and on another day, she was with Rhee, one of his Korean friends, but he was not suspicious; he loved her and trusted her. He looked forward to their happy future together.

He had given her fifteen thousand marks when he discovered she was pregnant. She claimed that Choi was the father, but Choi had not visited her in eight months; he had been in the hospital for four months and had spent another four months in treatment. Isabel did not know who the father was—Udo or Rhee. They would have to wait for the baby to be born before they could do blood tests to determine the father. That made the tragic affair worse.

Udo and Rhee wanted nothing to do with Isabel when she became pregnant; she had to carry the burden of the baby alone. Abortion was not possible in Germany; for that, she would have to travel to the Netherlands or Korea, but that was hard to decide. She was terrified and fearful of loneliness, Choi, and the future. She became so depressed that she went to the hospital.

When Choi came to visit, she was not in her room. He went to the hospital, where a Korean nurse who was a friend of Isabel told him everything. Choi was dumbfounded, but the worst news was that Isabel had used his money to buy a BMW that cost at least fifty thousand marks.

Choi tried to talk with Isabel, but she refused to see him. He came to me for help, but I could see no solution. I tried talking to her, but she just cried. I do not know about what—losing Choi's love? The baby? Her stupidity?

After that, I heard nothing about either of them until the police came to question me about my role in the matter. I had done nothing wrong, but they kept me in custody for almost two days. This was a problem that even Superman could not have solved. Choi and Isabel had both committed suicide. At least the police understood their backgrounds. What a terrible story.

Chapter 22

Why a Private Apartment?

Koreans in Germany met with accidents. Koreans tend to be sad, drink a lot, and indulge in nostalgia; they can think bleak and lonely thoughts. We Koreans had to deal with a traffic accident that caused the deaths of three of us, which drew us into an abyss.

Three of our comrades wanted to visit friends in Ahlen in Westphalia after midnight. They took a train and then a taxi. The accident occurred at a level crossing that was used only about ten times a year by trains. The warning signs all worked, so no one knows why the taxi driver crossed the tracks.

I was working as a master on the early shift. At eleven, the district overseer came and told me to call the police department.

"Police department? I'm not a criminal! Why again?"

The police asked me to come to the scene of the accident. They were trying to reconstruct the accident. I saw car parts. Flies were feasting on blood on the scraps of clothing I saw. The taxi driver had suffered only minor injuries. I could not shake the thought that he had intentionally killed the three Koreans.

Four weeks later, a hearing was held in court. The engineer told his story, a police officer testified that the hazard warning system was in order, and I identified the three victims. All in all, the procedure took just twenty minutes.

I took on the responsibility for the burials. I did not know who was who because the bodies were badly mangled. Two of the victims were friends of mine; they also had been saving money for further education. The third one I did not know because he had come to Germany after we had. One of the three, Kim, was married and had a one-year-old son. Kim had served in the military academy, where we had been officers. I knew his wife well. She wanted to work as a nurse in Dortmund; that was their plan.

The three had rented a private apartment because each of them had a girlfriend he wanted to entertain there. Two of the women were from Korea, while the third was a divorced German with a son. They had been traveling to their apartment.

All three were cremated together, and the ashes were divided. The ashes of two were sent to Korea while Kim's ashes stayed in Germany.

Three months after the funeral, Kim's wife came to Germany. She cried for two days with me, and she kept asking me why I had not prevented the arrangement about the private apartment, but I could not answer her. She complained to all his friends about it as well, but all of them were silent about her husband's girlfriend, who was a nurse at the hospital where she was working. If someone had mentioned that, it could have resulted in another tragedy.

Chapter 23

Petrified Jung

"Oh God, is poverty a sin? Where is my brother? How can I say goodbye to him? We were only two of us in the world! Our parents are already with you. I'm all alone now. How can I live alone? Oh God! Take me also with my brother. Ahh!"

The sister of Jung, my dear friend, was weeping over the ashes of her brother while we were on a boat in the Ruhr. She was next to the black box containing the ashes. She was in mourning clothes. With trembling hand, she tossed the ashes overboard. Actually, it was not his real ashes but powdered lime and ashes I had put together as we had not found her brother's body.

Jung, who was twenty-eight when he died, and his sister were orphans; their parents had been killed by terrorists. His father had worked in the Korean consulate in Kyoto, Japan, and had died when the children were only two and five. They grew up together, and they were very close.

Jung had trained in Korea to study abroad in Germany. His sister had worked as a nurse in Germany for some time and had advised him to study in Germany. He and I had trained together in Korea to work in Germany, and we worked together there. His German was as good as mine; we competed with each other to learn the language.

Workers were making repairs on a huge piece of equipment that mechanically cut coal off the face. Jung was in charge of handling the last, critical part of the procedure, which required him to crawl under the machine to unhook a chain. Just as he was doing that, the chain moved, and a link broke. That caused the other chains and guide bars to fall and bury Jung under an avalanche of steel.

The overseer above heard the thunderous noise. He called down but received no answer. He ordered the first master to alert the rescue squad.

I had gotten home at one that morning; I had drunk two bottles of beer and went to bed. I was asleep when I got the call. The vice director wanted me to come to the mine. My breath smelled of alcohol.

The rescue team tried to find Jung but could not. I formed a group to stabilize the coalface before we could move parts of the machinery. It took twenty-four hours. *What's happened to Jung? Is he alive? Where is he?*

He had been crushed beyond recognition. There was so little of his body that we could recover. In my mind, I could still hear his voice, but his soul had gone to heaven.

In his room, I found just traces of the human being. Letters from his sister. German language texts. His passbook had 13,600 marks, and in the pockets of his clothes were fifty-four marks. That was all I found of Jung. I could not cry, eat, sleep, study German—nothing. The idea that Jung was in heaven brought me peace.

I tried reaching his sister in West Berlin, but I learned she was in England and would not be back for a week. Without her, we could not have a funeral. Without a body, we needed no coffin. I dressed a mannequin in his best clothes. We put his coffin in the church until his sister arrived.

Sister Jung came a week after the accident. She had driven all night from Berlin and arrived at a quarter to five in the morning, completely exhausted. Shortly before I went to work at five thirty, I offered her a breakfast of tea, bread, and cheese. She fell asleep in my bed, and I went to work.

At work, I thought a lot about her. She was beautiful. She made my heart race. I had to tell myself again and again that she was the sister of my friend, not an object for my instinctual desire. I mentally asked the deceased to excuse my thoughts about his sister. I forgot Lala in Dusseldorf and my wife in Oxford. I thought only of Sister Jung.

I was on the bus going home at the end of the day. I was ashamed. I felt corrupted. A friend was dead, and all I could think of was my sexual desire for his sister. I felt like Dr. Jekyll and Mr. Hyde.

When I got to my place, Sister Jung looked at me and laughed. She pointed at my eyes. Embarrassed, I looked in the mirror. My eyebrows were buried in coal dust; I looked as if I had makeup on. I had been in such a hurry to see Sister Jung that I had not cleaned myself properly.

I gathered Jung's friends for a ten o'clock funeral at a Protestant church in Bochum. We cremated the remains. We were returning Jung's body to the fossils. In Korean, Jung means fossils.

We scattered the ashes in the Ruhr River. Sister Jung remained one more day. She thanked everyone who had known her brother. She whispered something in my ear, but I did not understand it. Was it just my wishful dream, or had she really said she loved me and wanted to come back to visit me?

Over time, memories of Jung faded from the minds of his Korean friends. Around mid-December, I received a letter from Sister Jung. She wanted to spend her two-week annual leave with me. I was hesitant to be unfaithful to Melanie, but I could not refuse Sister Jung's wishes. I decided that Sister Jung and I could travel as brother and sister. I bought two tickets to Rome, and I learned that Sister Jung was very cultured and knowledgeable. We did treat each other as brother and sister.

Part 6

The Determined Life

Chapter 24

A Third Journey

Of the Koreans who came with me to Germany, only forty-two of the forty-eight completed their three-year contracts. Only seven went directly back to Korea. Some founded schools of tae kwon do in different European countries. I went to some other mines and helped Koreans with their problems and with arranging to go home. Many of them needed my help as an interpreter.

We had learned German mining technology; usually, German miners had high school educations only, but most Koreans had bachelor's degrees. We could take the mining knowledge we gained back to help Korea.

Others from our group of forty-eight immigrated to the United States, England, Canada, Austria, France, and Spain. Two had died. Three had had serious accidents, and one ended up permanently handicapped. Three who graduated from the National Oceanography University in Pusan got jobs aboard ships in Bremen and Hamburg. Two opened a small business in Germany. And some in our group had married German women.

One of us worked at an Opel factory, and one who had studied to be a pharmacist in a Korean pharmacy found a job at Bayer. Four attended school to become nurses. Three opened restaurants in Hamburg, West Berlin, and Bonn. Two opened a travel agency in Frankfurt and Hamburg.

The one who had been fired for refusing to work became a millionaire in Paris by importing Korean food and then manufacturing it. He came up with a plan to attract French customers to his dumplings. He actually staged an accident with one of his trucks and scattered his dumplings filled with meat and vegetables all over the street. When the police and TV cameras arrived on the scene, he extolled the quality of his dumplings in perfect French—they were good for adults, and they would protect against cancer and all other diseases. He gave the reporters some samples to taste, and they praised his exotic Korean food highly. He was a sensation on the evening news, and orders began to flow in. He built a factory on the outskirts of Paris and became a millionaire.

Some others went to university. Ko, to whom I had taught English, attended New York University. One enrolled in Hamburg to study computer science. Others studied radiology at the University Karlsruhe, physics in Munich, Slavic languages in West Berlin, and Islamic studies in Hamburg. One remained in the Ruhr area and studied law in Bochum. Choi Abraham, who had studied economics in Korea, got a scholarship to the London School of Economics. Three others went to the College for Mines in Bochum.

The scalper invested in a tract of land that grew rapidly in value due to land speculation; he became a millionaire. One Kim opened a great restaurant in Seoul, and the other Kim bought a large cattle ranch in a province.

This story symbolizes the Korean character; the country had been through a proverbial hurricane, but the storm was passing and the sun was shining. It is the nature of Koreans to want the best for their children and give them good educations, and their children's desire for education is higher than that of other country's children. Private universities in Korea are nicknamed Cow Bones Towers, 牛骨塔, *woogoltab*. This is because it was common for peasants to sell off their cows and other livestock to pay for their children's education even if that meant they had to work their farms without the help of animals. Korea is a very small country. South Korea's young people have the potential to become highly educated and exceed in any field.

South Korea's economy has developed rapidly since the 1970s due to the resourcefulness of its youth and the seemingly infinite energy of its people.

Chapter 25

The Genius Melanie in Oxford

My wife passed the TOEFL as well as the Korean Examination of State for Study Abroad; both were very difficult exams, but she had a perfect score in the TOEFL and came out first in a group of two hundred in the other exam. Melanie is a genius.

We had not seen each other for two years. We were husband and wife, and we were finally going to be a couple. She flew from Korea to London, and I flew there from Dusseldorf and booked an expensive hotel—two hundred pounds for one night.

As I waited for her flight, I wondered what she would look like. My palms were sweating, and my mouth was dry. *What will I call her? You? My love? Darling? My sweetheart? Dear teacher? English teacher?* I did not know.

Among the first to leave the plane was a slim, tall woman with black hair. She was wearing an emerald-green dress. A fantastically beautiful woman. Because of her sunglasses, I did not know if she had seen me. I raised my hands. She did not see me. I waved again. *No, maybe that's not Melanie.* My legs were shaking. *It is Melanie, my wife! I'll call her Melanie, her Catholic baptismal name.*

"Melanie! Hello! Here I am. Hello! Melanie! Welcome to London! Thanks for coming. Thank you for loving me. Thank you for being my wife. Thank you!"

I waved at her, and she saw me and replied with a fond smile.

She could not wave because she had to carry two large suitcases and a handbag. Her white teeth flashed like stars. She looked like the princess in the movie *Roman Holiday.*

"Hello, my love! How are you?" she asked as she took off her glasses and hugged me. She smelled fresh and exciting. I was overjoyed, and she was crying for joy. We hugged. "Darling, I love you so much. You're my man. I want to be with you forever. I promise to live only for you. I'm in love with you. I'm so happy!"

"Melanie, we'll go directly to a hotel in London. Tomorrow morning, we will go to Oxford."

"Yes, my sweetheart."

"Melanie, you are very lovely and beautiful, a real princess. I love you, Melanie."

"Oh my dear, thank you!. My suitcases are filled with clothes I bought with the money you sent."

I grabbed a cart for the luggage, and we took a limousine to our hotel. We were sitting next to each other for the first time in our lives. I felt like I was flying, but at the same time, I was a little ashamed. Melanie just sat there quietly; I had no idea what she was thinking. Melanie was full of emotion, and I was too. We were finally together, and I felt elated, ecstatic. This is why men and women fall in love.

My princess had come to England to get a PhD with the full support of the Korean government. She had received a scholarship to study the English language and English didactic theory. She would study for three years, and that included finishing her doctoral thesis.

Melanie is my wife; I loved her wholeheartedly. I wanted to do everything for her that I could. She was worth it. She is a beautiful, smart, and wise partner, and I hoped we could pass that on to our children. She would succeed in her studies and go to a high place in life. I hoped the same for myself; it could mean wealth, honor, or even political power. But most important, we had a love that did not fear death.

We slept apart our first night, she in the expensive room at the Langham and I in a small, nearby hotel. We had not yet had a wedding ceremony that would make us a couple before God and our parents though we did have the appropriate papers. One day in a dream, Melanie had told me that we would lose our innocence together on our first night, and I had sworn that would happen. Although that would not be the case with me, I did not want to destroy her dream; I wanted pure Melanie to have a consecrated first night. I was sorry that I was not a virgin for her sake.

I remembered her quoting the Bible and telling me that the woman does not have authority over her own body; her husband did. She said the husband should fulfill his duty to his wife and the wife to her husband. They should not deprive each other of their company except perhaps by mutual consent for a time to pray, but then, they should return to one another so Satan would not tempt them.

Melanie often cited the first letter to the Corinthians, but the exact wording did not occur to me. Love is patient and kind, love is not jealous, not pompous, not flat, not rude. It does not seek its own interests; it is not quick-tempered; it does not brood over injury. It does not rejoice in wrongdoing but in truth. It bears all things, believes all things, hopes all things, and endures all things. Love never fails. Three important things are faith, hope, and love, and the greatest of these is love. I realized I had to act on these ideas in 1 Corinthians 13 for Melanie's sake.

Of course we could have slept together because we were married; that would not have been immoral, but Melanie wanted to wait until after the wedding ceremony. Is sexual intercourse before marriage a sin? The Bible says it is, and so does traditional Korean thinking. She and I were officially still courting. My experience with Lala had taught me about intimacy; it was difficult for me to lead an ascetic life and control my impulse. But I knew that Melanie wanted to wait, so that settled the matter. I had to follow her desires. I felt guilty for my sin with Lala, but I could not change that. I had not loved Lala; I had simply satisfied my desires with her, and Melanie's love for me was sincere.

I imagined Melanie's thoughts. *What should I do if my husband wants to sleep with me? Should I refuse? Should we proudly enjoy our first night together as a married couple? Joseph is not asking very much, but I wonder what he is thinking. He is a very gentle man. He is full of confidence. But maybe he considers this just a physical relationship?*

On the first night, a bride and a groom will naturally form a divine relationship with God's blessings. But they must respect each other and God's will. Melanie is precious, and I have to treat her like that. Our love will last a lifetime. Melanie is my first true love. For men, romance and marriage can be separate matters. I hope she will forgive my sins. She has a pure heart. I will cherish her forever.

The next day, we went to Oxford to register Melanie and meet her supervising professor, Sir Erwin Adam Hopkins; their meeting lasted an hour. The weather in Oxford was cool and rainy, but I was hot with tension. Nonetheless, everything went well. Melanie wasn't surprised at what he asked her to do to earn a PhD. She wanted to create a curriculum for teaching English to high school students in Korea, and she knew a lot about her subject. Sir Hopkins was very pleased. Melanie had told him that I was a student at a German university. She laughed and blushed when she told me that; it was at the time a lie.

Melanie was given a room in a dormitory. I complained about her room; I wanted her to have better living conditions for her studies even if I had to send her more money from Germany. She received a better room in a house. The landlady was a forty-eight-year-old woman, and five other foreign students lived there: Michiko from Japan, Maria from Mexico, Lucia from Ghana, Anne from South Africa, and Abdullah from Saudi Arabia. All except for Michiko were from royal families. Melanie's English was the best.

When students from abroad complete their studies at Oxford, they return to their homelands and are able to get good positions in foreign affairs; that improves relations between countries.

So my wife began her studies in Oxford. I went back to Germany a week later. While at Oxford, my wife was proud of me because my English was not bad and my German had become perfect. Princess Abdullah spoke good German and praised me several times. But we had to hide the fact that I was not at university. I vowed to get into graduate school in Germany within a year.

Chapter 26

Honeymoon Baby

Melanie was diligent in her studies. She participated in three advanced seminars and began to write her dissertation. She had three years to do that, but she wanted to finish in two and a half years.

I traveled to England when Melanie's mother came to visit. Melanie and I picked her up at the airport, and she looked very good even after the fourteen-hour flight. The women hugged each other and cried tears of joy.

"Let's talk about your wedding, Melanie," her mother said.

"Yes, Mother. I've arranged to be married at St. Paul's Cathedral in Oxford."

That was the first time I heard anything about being married in a cathedral, but we were married on a Sunday, and we went to Edinburgh, Scotland, on our honeymoon.

The first night, Melanie was very happy. She had kept her virginity, and we spent our first night together in wedded bliss. I felt guilty because of my past. I was embarrassed, but I could not change my situation. I vowed to be faithful to her and receive God's blessings. I hoped we would have a honeymoon baby.

We had a great time in Edinburgh. We stayed at a nice hotel and had wonderful meals. Melanie had gathered much information about Edinburgh, and we saw the Scott Memorial, which is a symbol of Edinburgh, Edinburgh Castle, the Royal Mile, Castle Hill, St.

Giles Cathedral, Ron Cannon Gate Market, Queen Elizabeth's Holyrood House Palace, and museums. We learned about Scotland's history and culture.

Our five-day honeymoon was memorable; Melanie's spiritual love was wonderful.

On the last night of the honeymoon, Melanie said, "Honey, I believe I'm pregnant."

"How on earth can you know that so soon?"

"I feel such joy of mind and body. I think we'll have a honeymoon baby."

"Melanie, I saw our baby in a dream."

"Honey, I did too! I'm really so happy."

At six o'clock the next morning, we went to the cathedral for Mass and went back to Oxford. My mother-in-law was very pleased.

Chapter 27

German Scholarship

I wanted to enroll as a graduate student. That was my reason for going to Germany in the first place. I signed a one-year extension on my work contract. I was supposed to work up until June 30, but I resigned a month early so I could study for the language exam

I stayed until the end of August 1974 at my same place; the mining company charged me five marks a day. There were few residents there. The home manager had served under Hitler in the navy and had lost a leg and an eye. He was a kind, gentle person and was always cheerful and industrious.

I studied German very diligently because I wanted to achieve the highest possible result. The university's language course started in October and ended on June 30. I reviewed all of the material I had about the German language. I ate only German food to save time, so my natural desire for Korean food had to remain unsatisfied. In order to keep body and mind in great shape, I walked daily for two hours. I learned thirty new words every day. For sixty days prior to the exam, I slept only from midnight to four; all the rest of the time, I studied.

Every Friday, I went to the university to collect material about the latest issues and trends about the Language for Hearing Test. Many foreign students were attending the German language summer course at the university; among them were seven Koreans. They mocked me for being a guest worker; they were all students who had come from Korea directly to Germany to study.

I met Paul, who was from Pakistan, in the cafeteria. He gave me a lot of material he had already mastered, and so I bought him lunch every Friday at the cafeteria, for which he was very grateful.

The Korean students gathered in the cafeteria on Fridays at one in the afternoon to talk about studies and about the problems at home. They often talked about the dictator Park and his iron and inhumane policy. When the conversation came around to him, all were furious; they were all patriots.

One Friday afternoon, the last day of instruction before the exam on the following Monday, a law student who had always ignored me told me he had a problem at the bank to which his mother had sent money for him. He needed to go to the bank, but he lacked day-to-day communication skills. His friends couldn't help him; they all wanted to study for the exam that weekend. He finally came to me. He looked very uncomfortable. His eyes spoke volumes. I watched him approach me out of the corner of my eye.

"Mr. Lee, I ask you for help," he asked sheepishly. He told me he needed me to go with him to the bank.

"Yes, Mr. Kim, if you will pay my traveling money."

Although I would have done it for free, I remembered my experience with the German who took my train fare.

"Thank you, Mr. Lee!"

We took the tram to the bank. His money had arrived a week earlier, but because of his poor language skills, there had been a misunderstanding. He had called to ask if the money had arrived but had not understood a word of the reply.

The language test was divided into two parts: a written part and an oral part. The written part covered dictation, retelling, and grammar. In dictation, we wrote five pages about a current problem that was dictated to us. Retelling was even more complicated; the ten-page text was about the conflicts in the Middle East. I could listen and understand, but I could not write that quickly.

The grammar part consisted of twenty-five questions; the questions about participial construction were difficult. Along with some additional written testing, the exam took six hours.

The oral examination took place a week later. Three women sat at a table and offered me my choice of three envelopes that contained questions I would answer orally. I chose one and handed it to her.

"You have selected a nice question, Mr. Lee," she said after she opened the envelope. "Here is the question: What is your opinion about the relationship between teachers and pupils? You have five minutes."

I had read some books about it written by Swiss philosopher Johann Heinrich Pestalozzi (1746–1827), kindergarten founder Friedrich Froebel (1782–1852), theologian Martin Buber (1878–1965), German philosophers Roth (1906–1983) and Theodor Litt (1880–1962), and a few others. So I began with what Buber had written. "The relationship between teachers and students is an educational relationship. It requires the love and trust God has given us."

I spoke in earnest about the technical pedagogical terms I had learned. "Pedagogical relations demand a lot of the teacher." I explained Plato's and Fichte's philosophies and the Socratic method. I mentioned Cicero's oratory, and I discussed the humanists' opinions of Dewey and Durkheim.

Finally, I mentioned the priesthood relationship in Korea explained by the concept of king-teacher-father, 君師父一體, *gunsabu ilze*. The teacher was in between the king and the father. "Teachers must model the values they want to teach their students; their importance cannot be overemphasized."

The exam was supposed to take twenty minutes, but after ten minutes, one woman said, "Enough, Mr. Lee. Wonderful." All three were very pleased and encouraged me with praise. They conversed with each other a few minutes. One said, "Dear Mr. Lee, you have been successful in this German examination, and we award you a one. In retelling, you have a two, but in dictating, grammar, and oral, you have all ones. We congratulate you for achieving the highest score of all those who took the test. Congratulations, and good luck with your studies."

The oldest woman shook my hand vigorously as the others smiled at me. I was floating on a cloud. I was very excited but a little depressed because I could not communicate the good news to my wife.

Of the seven Koreans, only four passed. Among those who had failed was the daughter of a famous professor of German in Korea. She would have to perhaps study in the United States.

After that, I sought acceptance into a PhD program. I wanted to study education. I spoke with Professor Hans Herbert Becker, and he was satisfied that I was prepared to work on a doctorate. I was given a government scholarship of two thousand marks per month, and I was then a graduate student as Melanie was. I will receive a scholarship of DM 2,000 per month from the German government in the future. Now it ensured equal status of Melanie.

As I drove my Volkswagen to the airport in Dusseldorf, I thought of the difficult years I had spent in the mines. When I saw the blue British Airways plane, my heart started beating rapidly. When we took off, I said, "Gluck auf!"

We humans exist in three states—wakefulness, dreamless sleep, and dreams. We have to understand how these are connected and interrelated. I had to prepare for a family with Melanie; that was my dream, and now I had to make it a reality during my waking hours.

When we landed at Heathrow, I saw Melanie in the arrival hall. She was crying. I wanted to tell her about my success with the German exam and my acceptance at the university so she would not have to worry about her lie to her professor. My mother-in-law took my hand. Melanie was still crying tears of joy, which are beautiful on Korean women, and Melanie was a Korean woman full of love and emotion. She was more beautiful than ever.

"Joseph, my son, my son-in-law, are you okay? Is your hard work over? I believe you will end up with a doctorate just like

Melanie. I bought a house in front of my house before coming here for you two."

"Mother, thank you. Enshrined mother, we'll live well. But it will take some time for us to finish our studies. After that, we will live in Seoul with you. And I have some very good news."

Melanie looked at me curiously.

"Mother, Melanie, I received a scholarship. I will be receiving two thousand marks monthly!"

"Really? Son-in-law, I am so happy. Wonderful! Magnificent! Splendid."

Melanie didn't have a taste for food because she was pregnant. She had gotten her degree, and she still had half a year on her Korean scholarship. I suggested that she go to the United States to study more and have the baby there so our child would become a citizen. After thinking about it, Melanie agreed, and she and her mother went to New York.

Three months later, Melanie went to the New York University Hospital to deliver our child. I flew there hastily. Melanie gave birth to a son. Melanie smiled and named him Luke.

Four weeks later, Melanie, Luke, and Luke's grandmother flew to Seoul.

Chapter 28

Das Rigorosum and Back to Korea

I returned to Germany. My dissertation title was "German Preservice Gymnasium Teacher Education and the Preservice Secondary Teacher Education in Korea—A Comparative Study."

As far as my dissertation was concerned, I had done well. I had to correct some grammar problems, but I received help with that.

My dissertation was accepted, but I had to pass an oral exam. Three professors would ask me questions on my research for two hours; this oral exam was rigorous. It would be my last test ever. But it would be hard. The professors all had different attitudes toward pedagogy. I was sweating, but I received ones, the highest marks, from all of them.

After two hundred copies of my dissertation were sent to university libraries, I was awarded a doctorate. It had taken me two and a half years. I proudly returned to Korea.

I took a position in the National Research Institute of Education (NRIE) with Melanie's encouragement. She had asked the dean at her university to hire me, but the policy was to not have married couples on the same faculty. Thus, I took this research position to help the government reform education in the country. My status at the NRIE was equivalent to that of a full professor at a state university. And Melanie gained tenure at her university.

All's well that ends well. The results are important, but so is the process.